THE *Angler's Companion*

THE *Angler's Companion*

Sara Godwin

Top Fishing Holes, Classic Literature, Fish Tales, Equipment, & Much More Fun from the World of Fishing

MALLARD PRESS
An imprint of BDD Promotional Book Company, Inc.
666 Fifth Avenue
New York, New York 10103

A FRIEDMAN GROUP BOOK

Published by MALLARD PRESS
An imprint of BDD Promotional Book Company, Inc.
666 Fifth Avenue
New York, New York 10103

Mallard Press and its accompanying design and logo are trademarks of BDD
Promotional Book Company, Inc.

Copyright ©1991 by Michael Friedman Publishing Group, Inc.

First published in the United States of America in 1991 by
Mallard Press.

ISBN 0-7924-5306-9

THE ANGLER'S COMPANION
Top Fishing Holes, Classic Literature, Fish Tales, Equipment, and Much More
from the World of Fishing
was prepared and produced by
Michael Friedman Publishing Group, Inc.
15 West 26th Street
New York, New York 10010

Editor: Elizabeth Viscott Sullivan

Art Director: Jeff Batzli

Designer: Edward Noriega

Photo Researcher: Daniella Jo Nilva

All illustrations © Ron Pittard/Courtesy Windsor Publications

Typeset by: M&M Typographers, Inc.

Color separations by Scantrans Pte. Ltd.

Printed and bound in Singapore by Tien Wah Press Pte. Ltd.

Table of Contents

DEDICATION

To my father,
Robert Franklin Godwin II,
who made me dig my
own worms as a
lesson in self-reliance,
and to John True,
who persuaded me to
the pleasures of angling
with a fly.

ACKNOWLEDGEMENTS

I must extend my heartfelt appreciation to Jon Ray, the world champion tournament fly caster who spent hours teaching me to fly cast; to John McCosker, Director, Steinhardt Aquarium, San Francisco, California, who always made time to answer my questions: to Paul Wulf and Peter Wooley who sorted out the flies and fly-fishing tackle for me, and Gene Fassi who did the same for spin-casting gear. My thanks, too, to all those who have helped me fish my way across Canada, including Jim Norwood of Tourism Canada; Jerry Bricker of Frontier Lodge, Great Slave Lake, Northwest Territory; George and Marion Peacock and Jack and Pat Austad, Whitehorse, Yukon; Cliff Blackmuir of Otherside Lodge, Lake Athabasca, Saskatchewan; Peter Chernier, Calgary, Alberta; Brian and Sharon Elder of Woollaston Lake Lodge, Lake Woollaston, Saskatchewan; Russ Johnson and Keith Fraser of North Pacific Springs Lodge, Duncan, British Columbia; Pond's Chalet, Miramichi River, New Brunswick; and Fair Gordon, who took me ice fishing on Lac Chibougamau, Quebec. A special thanks to Dick Powers of Whaler's Cove Lodge, Angoon, Alaska, where my husband found out what extraordinary fishing is all about, and to Elton Welke, fly fisherman *par excellence*, who gave me Ernest Schwiebert's *Trout* (two volumes) as a wedding present. To all of these, my deepest gratitude for their time and knowledge, and their generosity in sharing both with me. Any errors, God forbid, are exclusively my own.

CHAPTER ONE

The Gentle Art

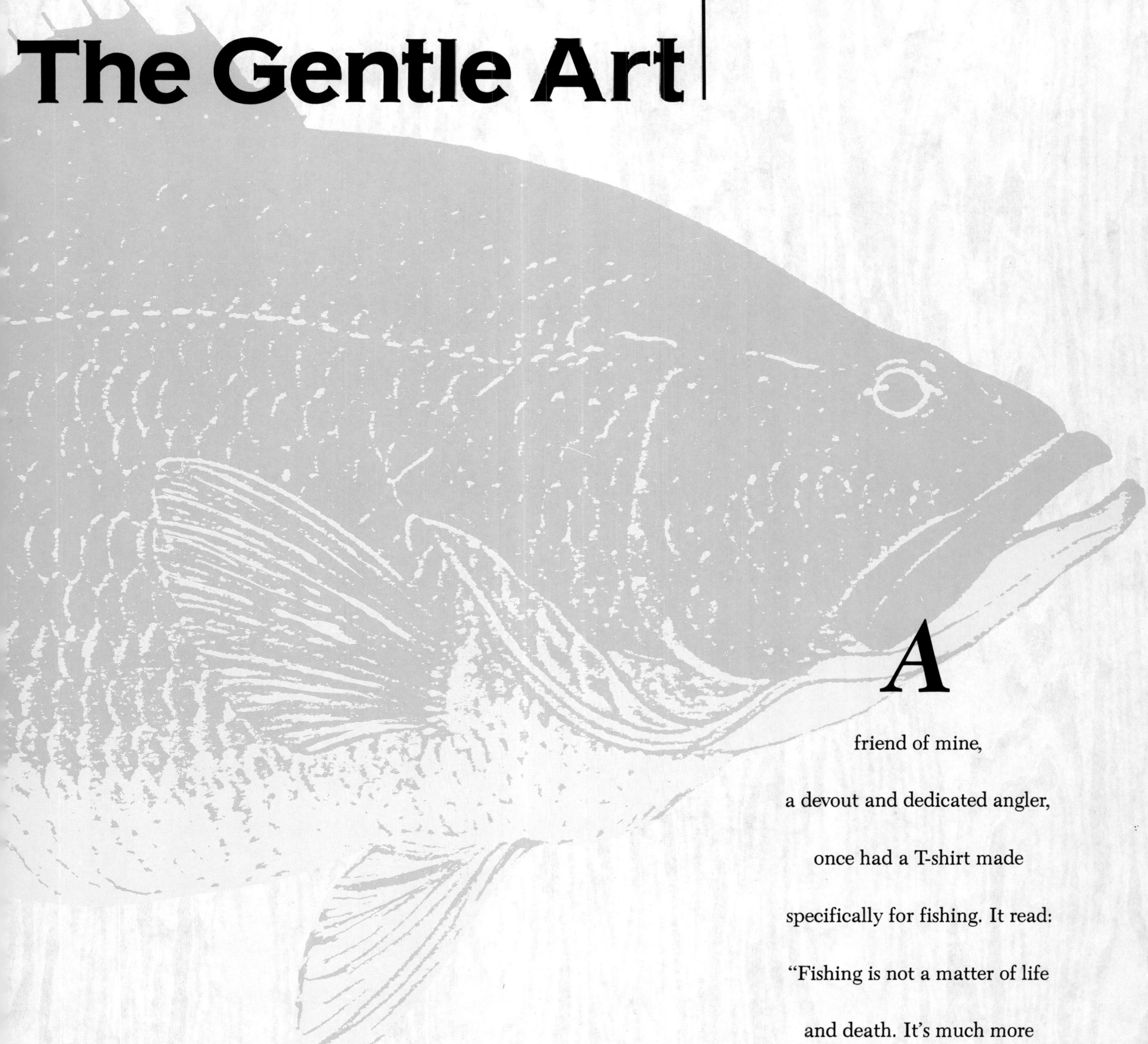

A friend of mine, a devout and dedicated angler, once had a T-shirt made specifically for fishing. It read: "Fishing is not a matter of life and death. It's much more important." That understanding of the Zen of fishing, that clear perception of proper priorities, has always struck me as being both perfect and precise.

Fishing is much more than merely catching fish. For one thing, it is the quiet pleasure of preparing all the "gear and tackle and trim," as the poet Gerard Manley Hopkins put it, the unclouded happiness of anticipation. There is the warmth of the sun, the mist rising off a silvered lake, the song of a clear-running stream, the dazzling play of light on the water, and the shining scales of the fish, all apart from the fun of catching and eating the fish. In the hush of a forest, with no sounds but the wind through the trees and birdsong, there comes the chance to puzzle out one's purpose on the planet. In these places there is a solitude, a silence, a solace seldom found on urban pavements. Of this quiet and contemplation and the practice of "the gentle art," as Isaac Walton called fishing, only good can come.

Angler's Disease

THE symptoms are universal: a certain preoccupied air, a peculiar shambling gait, as though the victims were not in full possession of their faculties. Muttering softly, they repeat strange incantations, words scarcely comprehensible to the ear of those not equally afflicted: lures, leaders, lines. One fears for their poor minds. The sickness is tied, inexplicably, to the seasons. With the first breath of spring, the first snowmelt in the streams, the victim is gripped by a trembling palsy of the hands, a manic eagerness. With killing swiftness, comes the final symptom: abandoning career, deserting family and friends, the victim wanders off into the wilderness, not to be seen again by loved ones until the madness passes. And pass it will, for fishing season does close come fall, and the sorry angler returns once more to home and hearth, to spend another year until fishing season opens, and the mania strikes again.

Is there help for those thus affected? No. It is a lifelong disease with no known cure. It may be congenital: There are those who

OPPOSITE PAGE: Morning mist, the boat adrift, a lone fisherman looking for that first fish.

© Betty Groskin

ABOVE: An autumn afternoon spent intriguing and enticing trout.

OPPOSITE PAGE: The boy's eyes are glued to the bobber; the sun is warm on his back...any second a fish might take the bait....

have declared themselves born fishermen. It can certainly be terminal, for many are those who fished until the day they died. The pharmaceutical industry has yet to find the key to even a remission of the symptoms. Millions are stricken, and the lives of many millions more are touched by watching the inevitable progress of the disease in those they love, but does the government provide a subsidy for those thus afflicted? Not one red cent.

Today, millions of men, women, and children go fishing for the pure fun of it every year. Their numbers continue to grow steadily as more and more people seek the solace, silence, and soul-cleansing that only the out-of-doors and wilderness can provide.

The trend is clear: neither rain nor sleet nor snow nor dark of night can keep the angler from discovering every corner where fish can be caught. I, and others of my ilk, rise before the light of day, gulp scalding liquids to jar ourselves into a state of consciousness, or a reasonable facsimile thereof, carry mountains of gear to the car, and drive for hours on roads apparently devoid of human life, just to go fishing.

I was extremely wise in my choice of parents: within a few months of my birth, they moved to the West Coast of the United States and I have never lived more than an hour from the ocean and its fish in my entire life. Childhood summers were spent fishing at my grandfather's summer place at Minocqua in northern Wisconsin. My father undertook my education as an angler with tutorials that began with a green handline wound on a red wooden frame. It was an inviolable injunction that I dig my own worms and bait my own hook, and on that glorious occasion when I actually caught some inexplicably suicidal perch or bluegill, I cleaned my own catch under the supervision of my father's expert eye. I progressed in time from panfish to bass and pike and trout, from the little handline to a white fiberglass rod, magnificent to my ten-year-old eyes. (Somehow my father accidentally left that rod behind in Grand Central train station in Chicago on the way home. I mourn it still.) When at last I attained my maturity, I left my childhood home to move even closer to good steelhead and salmon fishing.

What is it that lures one to this insanity? Is it a fascination with the toys and trinkets of tackle? Heaven knows, the assortment of rods, reels, lines, leaders, and lures is endless. Is it the sap-rising of spring, this craving to be out-of-doors? Certainly, opening day finds fishermen bumper-to-bumper on the backcountry roads, gunwale-to-gunwale on the lakes, elbow-to-elbow on the streams. Is it the primal urge of the hunter to bring home food for the family? That seems scarcely possible, since the job could be done better and cheaper at a supermarket. Is it the sun warm on one's back, or the camaraderie of boon companions, or the moments of silence and

Only a few more minutes of fishing before the squall hits.

© Jeff Greenberg

Two fishing buddies with fine stringers of fish—just the sort of thing required for a hearty campfire meal.

solitude? Is it the sheer beauty of the fish themselves, drawn glistening and iridescent from the shining waters, with bright colors shimmering on their scales? Or is it merely madness that makes a person slog through tangled underbrush, wrestle with a recalcitrant outboard motor, spend all day fishing and often have little or nothing to show for their pains besides a sunburned nose? A sound, solid case might be made for simple mania. But the case isn't airtight, and a great many people have argued eloquently and persuasively that a passion for fishing bespeaks a finer form of sanity than is often found in our common round.

It is curious that a number of those who have sought to make the case for fishing make their livings in daily disputation: Robert Traver was a judge in Michigan when he wrote the classic *Trout Madness*. The sub-title of *Trout Madness* is *A Dissertation on the Symptoms and Pathology of This Incurable Disease by One of Its Victims*. Roderick Haig-Brown was a Judge of the Provincial Court of British Columbia and Chancellor of the University of Victoria when he wrote *A River Never Sleeps*. Haig-Brown doesn't dwell long on the disease itself; he chooses instead to write about the joys of fishing every month of the year, and to expound long and lyrically on what he caught, where he caught it, and what he caught it on. Perhaps one might say that he demonstrates the progressive nature of the disease, the symptoms and obsession growing worse with each passing year. Or perhaps the increasing symptoms of insanity derive from the fact that anglers hear all too clearly the footsteps of passing time, the intimations of mortality. One day we will no longer be able to climb down the steep, slippery bank to the best fishing hole we know; one day the current may be too swift for us to wade; or the fisherman's ultimate nightmare, the unutterable horror, that one day we will hook a fish too big to play.

Fleeing these fears with the eagerness and enthusiasm that only true terror can lend the legs, fishermen become charter subscribers to the notion of *carpe diem*. Taking to heart Robert Herrick's admonition to gather rosebuds while they may (or more accurately, fish while they can), in full cognizance that old Time is still a-flying, they disappear every day of fishing season that they can slip the bonds of life, loved ones, and work.

Like the wanton and wayward of an earlier era, the avid angler is more to be pitied than censured. Spring entices with its soft, seductive warmth. Each dormant root re-enacts the resurrection. Every walk in the woods is nothing less than an act of pagan wor-

Some things just seem to go naturally with fishing—a big straw hat on your head and a big dog at your feet.

ship. And the fish rise, lean and hungry, from the dark depths to feast upon *Ephemera* (May flys). Who could resist such blandishments? Surely, it was a better time when our lives were in tune with the seasons, and the angler who braved the sharp, rushing waters to bring home the first fresh fish was greeted and honored as a hero, not held in contempt as a ne'er-do-well.

Serious anglers, as Izaak Walton observed, are essentially contemplative souls. It takes little to bring them joy: a catalog of fishing gear and tackle to peruse on a quiet evening, the sun rising over the water as they rig their rods, the comfortable companionship of fellow anglers when the day is done.

Somehow the smell of coffee brewing and bacon sizzling (two things I don't normally consume at all) is more tantalizing on the days I go fishing. I love rummaging through my tackle and making thoughtful, considered decisions about which rod, which reel, which line is absolutely essential. My fishing friends often wonder aloud at this thoughtful deliberation, cruelly pointing out that, in the end, I take everything I own anyway. It is, I protest, only wisdom to do so. If there's a wind, it's nigh unto impossible to fly fish, so of course I need the spinning gear as well. And if a lake is our agreed destination, it's entirely possible, nay, even probable, that we will pass by an inviting stream or two. Should such a thing come to pass, how could I forgive myself if I failed to take my waders? And if the weather is fine on the lake, a swimsuit is definitely required. And lures in several sizes and...well, you understand.

All this is merely the pleasure of anticipation. A joy itself, it is as nothing compared to the galvanizing *frisson* of a solid strike, that unique combination of fear and delight when I know for a certainty there's a good fish on. Part of the pleasure is in making the strike; another fair portion is in playing the fish. I fish mostly catch-and-release these days, and so there is a certain satisfaction, too, having fought and won, in sparing a fine fish to fight another day.

The infinite variety may be why fishing never palls for me. Every stream, river, lake, bay, and ocean is different. Every species of fish, each type of tackle, holds its own fascination. I have fished for king salmon and brought home three fish that together weighed more than I did. I have fished for humpbacked salmon (pinks) on days when, with four rods out, all four had fish on. I once saw a pike so big, so fierce, it snapped a steel leader like a piece of thread. I've reeled up halibut that felt as though I'd caught a waterlogged mattress and the halibut wasn't even all that big. A sixteen-pound (7-kg) chum (dog salmon) took a Black Woolly Bugger fly at the mouth of an Alaskan stream, and promptly headed back out to sea. I lost that fish to a broken hook, but it went with my blessings, for it had given me a glorious hour of reel-singing fight that I daydream of again and again. What else on earth is there, except possibly great sex, that gives one such unadulterated pleasure in the anticipation, the act, and the savoring of memories?

A fishing companion is not to be chosen casually or carelessly. First, this sterling individual must be available to go fishing when you are, and must know enough not to tell everyone where your favorite fishing hole is. Next, he or she must be essentially compatible: those who hold seriously opposed views on the traditionally controversial issues—economics, politics, and religion—are best left behind unless you are of the conviction that pleasant conversation and embattled disputation are synonomous. Last, and most important, your companion must approach fishing with the same level of fervor with which you yourself approach the sport. Few projects are more cer-

© Jeff Greenberg

OPPOSITE PAGE: *Two friends in a moment of reflection.*

ABOVE: *Mom! Dad! Look what we caught this morning! Can we have 'em for dinner? Please?*

On the Selection of Fishing Buddies

© Peter Hong

Perhaps every adult's favorite memory, and every child's favorite moment, is fishing off the dock at a summer home on the lake.

tainly condemned to failure than the fishing trip undertaken by one who believes fishing is a matter of baiting a hook, tossing a line into the water and devoting full attention to a comfortable nap and another who is convinced that fishing is a matter of outwitting the fish, best accomplished by stalking, belly to the ground, through thick underbrush to an overgrown overhang where he may dap undetected by human or beast. The person who likes to bet on who will catch the biggest or the most fish is not a good mix with the gentle soul who doesn't remember how many he caught or even know exactly what they were.

Skill counts, too. I was once assigned a fishing partner at Frontier Lodge on Great Slave Lake in Canada's Northwest Territories, a young man named Tom, who had come to the Lodge with his parents. Over the first few days Tom and I consistently came back with more and bigger fish than his mother and father caught. Tom was a pleasant, soft-spoken fellow, an intelligent and thoughtful

A quiet afternoon spent still fishing.

fisherman, and a pleasure to fish with. One evening his mother announced that she wanted to fish with him the next day. Tom gave this his usual serious consideration, and then said, "No, I'd rather fish with Sara. She can tie her own knots." Over the years, I have been given various compliments that I have treasured gratefully for years. His is among them.

OBVIOUSLY, the best fishing companion is one precisely designed to one's own liking, rather than "off the rack," as it were. Small children often work very well for this, for as the twig is bent, so grows the tree. If one wishes a little bait fisherman, why, children may be taught at a very early age to dig earthworms. If one wishes a tiny trout angler, there is no better way to start than one of the many trout farms that can be found all over the country. I once took my son to such a place. He was only six or seven, but one cannot

On the Delicate Art of Developing a Companion of One's Own

begin too early to inculcate proper values in one's offspring. The proprietor rented us all the necessary tackle, and the trout pond positively swarmed with rising fish. While we were there, some far-sighted papa was seeing to his daughter's angling education by celebrating her birthday with a fishing party, along with some ten or twelve other young ladies. They were catching fish as fast as they could reel them in, and I have no doubt that his daughter is today an accomplished angler.

My son, however, couldn't quite get the knack of it. I showed him how to watch the tip of his rod—a wiggle means a nibble, I instructed. I demonstrated a strike, and caught a fish in the process. I did it several times over, but still the lessons didn't seem to take.

The blue sky clouded over, and a chill wind drove the little girls in their party dresses away. Josh kept fishing. The party set had their fish weighed and counted and cleaned. Josh set his jaw, and kept fishing. It began to drizzle miserably, and I suggested, very gently, that we might try again another day. Josh kept fishing more fiercely than ever.

And suddenly he had a fish and it didn't jump free and he had it at his feet and it was a fine, fat trout, bigger than any I had caught in my attempts at teaching. We had it weighed and cleaned and took our leave. I turned on the heater in the car as high as it would go—we were both soaked through—and Josh spent the long ride home explaining to me how to catch the big ones.

Attempting to make an angler of an adult is a trickier business, the difference in difficulty between planting a seedling and training an espalier. Where enthusiasm alone may serve for the one, the other requires a dedicated and delicate diplomacy. For many years I took my fishing trips alone, taking potluck on fishing partners at various fish camps and lodges. My husband had expressed a distinct

© Kenneth Martin/Amstock

OPPOSITE PAGE: *The fisherman's pride—a fine mess of fish and the rod that landed them. Here is lunch on its way to happen.*

ABOVE: *Grandpa shows the kids how to fish the Cape Cod herring run, a Massachusetts tradition that pre-dates the Pilgrims.*

dislike for being cold and wet, and the idea that a fish might not take his hook as soon as it hit the water offended him mightily. To say he took it personally is an understatement approaching prevarication. It was obvious that he needed an introduction to the pure fun of fishing.

Whaler's Cove Lodge off Admiralty Island in southeastern Alaska seemed the perfect solution: the brochure guarantees the fishing. If you're not satisfied after two days, your money is re-funded in full, and owner Dick Powers says he's never had anyone take him up on it. This, clearly, was the place to take a belligerent beginner. We caught salmon, mostly pinks, some silvers, and a couple of kings. We caught our limit of halibut. We caught trophy-size Dolly Varden, and watched a couple of huge chums take a Black Woolly Bugger fly.

The last day we fished with a high school football coach from Denver and his son. There were four rods out and for an entire day, we didn't go more than ten minutes without a fish on. At one point there were four fish on, the captain of our boat was working desper-ately to keep the lines out of the kelp beds, and all four anglers were slipping and sliding all over the deck, yelling madly for the landing net. Suddenly a big halibut, previously dispatched to the fish box, gave his tail a mighty flick, sent the top of the box flying, and flipped itself onto the deck where it flopped wildly, contributing its might to the general clamor and confusion.

The story has a happy ending: we recaptured the halibut, my husband chasing it around the deck with the priest until the stun-ning blow was applied, and we landed all four salmon. In five days of fishing he and I released three-quarters of what we caught, and still brought home 175 pounds (79 kg) of salmon. He likes fishing much better now.

The best part of fishing—those quiet moments of contemplation on the ways of the world and the mysteries of fish.

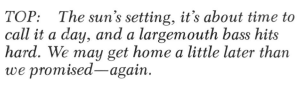

TOP: *The sun's setting, it's about time to call it a day, and a largemouth bass hits hard. We may get home a little later than we promised—again.*

BOTTOM: *Lake trout like this handsome fellow are cold water fish, which grow only about an inch (25 mm) a year.*

CHAPTER TWO

Begin with the Fish

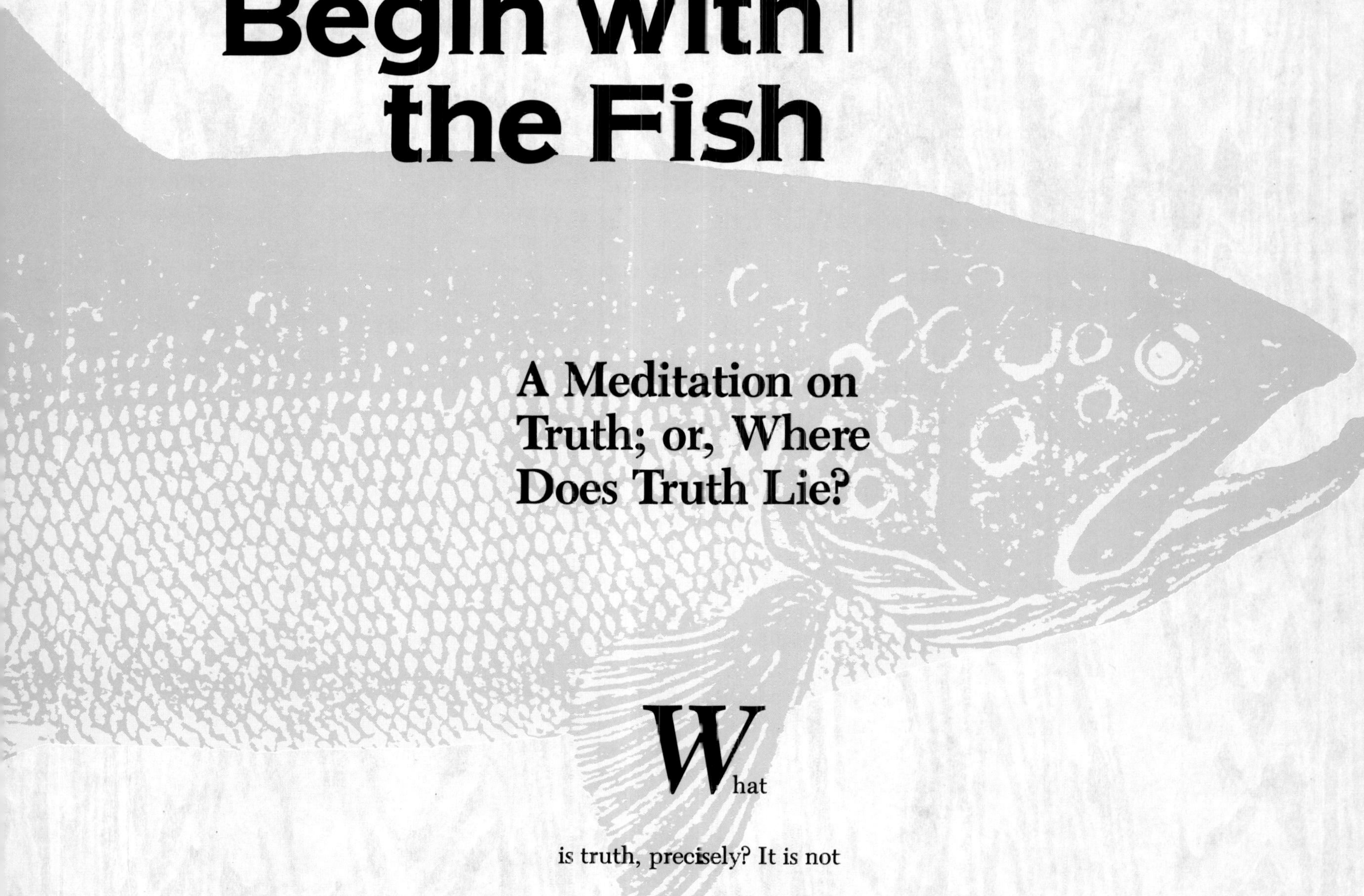

A Meditation on Truth; or, Where Does Truth Lie?

hat

is truth, precisely? It is not

mere accuracy. That would be the

equivalent of suggesting that

because both the drifting dunes

of the Sahara and the

wave-lapped beaches of Bali

are indisputably composed

of sand, that they are identical.

Scientists may expound at length

(and they do, they do) about

how many scales a certain

species of fish has,

Those recurved teeth are the reason guides hate catching pike. It's easy enough to get your hand into retrieve the lure; the problem is getting it back out again.

how many teeth and how they are arranged, the precise position of the dorsal and lateral fins, and in the end, they would not have said one word that was untrue nor would they have fully described the fish.

What of the truth of the poet, who tells of the river's sinuous silver flow, the sunlight dancing on the ripples, the fascination of the dark ellipse of a fish's shadow? The poet is no less accurate than the scientist, but neither has told the entire truth.

What, then, of the anglers, whose fish was strong and noble, whose tackle creaked and groaned under the strain, who saw, with their own eyes, the scales flash silver and gold as the fish leaped for the sun, as though it would trade Neptune for Apollo.

If truth is more than precise accuracy, more than pure poetry, more than experience and emotion, how shall it be comprehended in a single tale? Has the angler told less of the truth than the scientist and the poet? Or more?

The Angler's Truth

FISHERMEN are not famous for their simple honesty. In fact, if truth be told, they are more widely known for a certain evasiveness, a certain ineluctable uncertainty as to the limitations of demonstrable fact. Traditionally, fish grow longer and heavier with each telling of the tale, fish lost are always bigger than those brought home. But there is another aspect to it, rather more sinister than the natural exaggeration of the sportsman. Ask anglers what their favorite lure is, and you'd best have plenty of time to listen; ask where their favorite fishing hole is, and full-grown human beings are suddenly and inexplicably reduced to the awkward reticence of embarrassed adolescents.

There is something fiercely private about fishing, something that justifies in the angler's mind, the web of elaborate half-truths and outright lies they tell. The web is woven for strangers and dear friends alike. The person who fishes for trophy marlin may tell you that the fish was caught off San Jose del Cabo in the Gulf of California, but will never reveal how precisely far off Punta Gorda it was. Those individuals who fish mostly to escape the urban grind will stop on the way home at a supermarket and buy trout sooner than admit that they took all their tackle out only to walk in the woods the whole day. The man who slipped away to avoid a personal confrontation with his front lawn will handle smelly, slimy bait for hours in order to bring home fish that will allow him to think of himself as a good family provider instead of as a man who avoids the yardwork.

The trees have turned, the water's as smooth as glass—one last perfect day of fishing before winter closes in.

The old "Gone Fishin'" sign is not a sign of admirable enterprise. It is the sign of the sneak, the shirker, the loafer. Because it is perceived thus, the fisherman is forced to lie. I was once blessed with a freelance assignment to write a magazine article about a floating fishing lodge in British Columbia. Pleased, in fact delighted, I took the vacation time I'd earned from my corporate job, had the art director make me a properly crooked "Gone Fishin'" sign, hung it on my office door, and headed north for some trophy salmon fishing. When I came back, the sign had disappeared. A worried colleague had removed it for fear upper management would not be amused. So it is that society, while deploring the fisherman's lies, allows us no choice but to tell them.

NOT only is the fisherman probably less than perfectly straightforward, and certainly capable of sidestepping issues, but is a snob as well. No Brahmin ever beheld an Untouchable with more distaste than the fly fisherman regards those who fish with bait. The bait fisherman, in turn shrugs and points out that Izaak Walton, whom the flycaster holds holy, was himself a bait fisherman, and used live bait at that. With a fine string of fish to show for their efforts—as opposed to a box of pretty flies—those who fish with bait have no complaint, though they may well believe that the fly fisherman's tendency to flog the water puts down the fish in an unconscionable manner.

There are many castes in any society, of course. Just as the Hindus have their scholars, warriors, merchants, and menials, just as every high school has its brains, jocks, and geeks, no less finely are the lines drawn among fishermen. Do you fly fish or spin cast? Do you fish wets or drys? Can you tell a Mayfly from a stonefly, a

On the Delicate Subject of Snobbery

OPPOSITE PAGE: Lizard Lake at Marble, Colorado, offers fine trout fishing in some of the most beautiful country in North America. The Frying Pan River that runs through nearby Redstone is one of Colorado's best trout streams.

ABOVE: A deep-diving lure takes good walleye as the net attests; walleye like to skulk in deep water.

Good trout water at the foot of the Maroon Bells near Aspen, Colorado. The scenery in reality and in reflection is so spectacular it competes with the trout for even the most devout angler's attention.

BELOW: This rainbow trout came with bragging rights attached.

OPPOSITE PAGE, NEAR RIGHT: Golden trout, found only at high elevations, qualify as a trophy on the basis of rarity alone. This one was caught and released in a lake in the Wind River Range in Wyoming.

OPPOSITE PAGE, FAR RIGHT: Trout fishing in the Canadian Rockies is superb. This is Herbert Lake near Banff, Alberta.

A Meditation on Fish

bivisible from a nymph? Do you use lures or bait? Is the bait live or dead? Do you use natural baits like the time-honored worm or cheese and bacon spiced with your personal secret ingredient? Do you backpack thirty-five miles (56 km) into the wilderness to pursue the elusive golden trout or take out the bass boat with its 150 hp Mercury to bring back black bass from the local reservoir? Do you read the water and work it, pool, eddy, and riffle, or do you always fish off the same sunken log you've fished off for so many years the boat knows the way by itself?

Do these distinctions seem a bit arcane? Ah, beware, beware my friend. Only put the person who fishes with rods of Tonkin cane and a monogrammed silver flask of good Scotch, next to the simple soul who fishes with a quart of grasshoppers and a jug of homebrew, and you will see with your own eyes what produced the Marxist dialectic. Marx would probably protest that the social, political, and economic implications of *Das Kapital* were based on far more solid issues than mere snobbery, on more than the aristocracy's disdain of the proletariat, more than the proletariat's dismissal of the peasant, more than the peasantry's hatred of both, but he'd be hard pressed to prove it.

BUT enough of the fisherman; what of the fish? If fishermen seem a slippery sort, their quarry is no better. Let us look for a moment at the trout. The trouble with trout is that one never knows when a trout *is* a trout. A trout may be a true trout or a salmon or a char. All of them are salmonids, a big word which means "related to salmon." There are brook trout and brown trout, golden trout and rainbow trout, lake trout and sea trout. The brook trout, also called "speckles" for its (did you guess?) speckles, is *Salvelinus fontinalis*, a name which scarcely lessens the confusion, since it means "little salmon that lives in brooks." Along the eastern seaboard, they migrate to the sea and return as sea trout, all of which sounds perfectly straightforward until you find out that the weakfish is also called sea trout, and it is a complete imposter, not even vaguely related to the salmonid family.

But that's not the worst of it: the brook trout is not, in fact, a trout at all, but a char like its cousins the lake trout (also known as Mackinaw, grey trout, and togue), the Dolly Varden, and the Arctic char. How to tell the difference? The scales are easy to see on true trout, looking rather like an iridescent medieval chain mail. On char, the scales are extremely small and so deeply and closely set as to look more like skin than scales.

On the Pacific Coast from northern California to Alaska, anadromous rainbow trout migrate out to sea from the coastal streams and rivers, and when they return, are called steelhead, *Salmo gairdnerii*. Landlocked rainbows, found in lakes or rivers now blocked by impassable dams, are simply called rainbows, *Salmo irideus*.

TOP: Rainbow trout are native to North America, but they are recognized world-wide as one of the finest game fish. They have been successfully transplanted to Africa, South America, and New Zealand, where they often grow much larger than at home.

MIDDLE: Golden trout are found only at high elevations in the Sierra Nevada and Rocky Mountains. They have rarely trans-planted successfully to lower elevations.

BOTTOM: Cutthroat trout were discovered by the Lewis and Clark Expedition (1803-1806), and named after William Clark. The expedition explored from the Mississippi River at St. Louis, Missouri, west to the mouth of the mighty Columbia River.

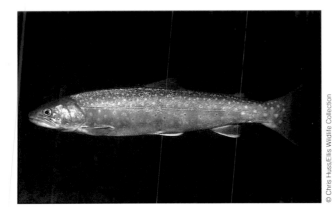

Cutthroat trout, distinguished by the slash of bright red along the lower jaw that makes each one look as though it's been mugged by Mack the Knife, were found by the Lewis and Clark Expedition in the early 1800s, and christened *Salmo clarkii*.

The rarest of the trout is the golden trout (*Salmo aquabonita*), named not for the manner in which it is valued, though that would be entirely appropriate, but for its brilliant yellow markings. As a work of art, the golden trout is nothing short of spectacular. It has a dark green back with even darker sports, a broad band of red with blue patches on the sides, bright gold on the belly and lower sides, and the whole finished off with crimson gills and belly fins. Identification is seldom a problem.

Golden trout are found exclusively in small, remote, high-altitude lakes in California's Sierra Nevada and the Rocky Mountains. To get to them means packing in, on horseback or backpacking. Which is to say, few folks catch golden trout by accident. Most of the anglers who catch golden trout do so because they plotted and planned and

hoped and prayed for the moment when a golden trout would take
their hook, and not because they just happened to be meandering
about in the mountains above six thousand feet (1,800 m), miles from
civilization, and thought they'd try casting a few.

The golden trout is prized because of its rarity, not its size; few
get as big as twelve inches (30 cm). They have not transplanted well,
either in lakes at the altitudes where they are typically found or in
larger lakes at lower elevations. The few that have survived at lower
elevations have responded to the warmer waters and more food by
growing larger than usual, some to more than ten pounds (4.5 kg).

By all reports, they are not difficult to catch: they come eagerly
to the fly or a small lure. They feed and spawn in the few months
between the breakup of the ice in June or July and October, when
the lakes freeze hard again. Golden trout are small because food is
not abundant in the tiny lakes in which they live, and they are
generally hungry enough to strike quickly at anything that might be
food, which makes the action fast and fun.

*What more could a boy want than his very
own fly rod, a pair of waders, and good
trout water to fish on the Connetquot
River, Long Island, New York.*

The Gallant Grayling

An Arctic grayling.

© Tony Mandile

ARCTIC grayling (*Thymallus signifer*), native to northern Canada, are often discussed in the same breath with trout, not because they are related, but because they give the angler a similar sort of fight. There is none of the stealthy stalking that's required to take a brown trout. There is none of the business of enticing the fish hidden beneath an undercut streambank as with rainbows. There is none of the endless trolling to find the precise depth at which the salmon are feeding that day. No, the Arctic grayling rises easily to either fly or lure, fights gallantly, leaps often, and once landed, is startlingly beautiful.

I caught my first Arctic grayling in the rapids of the Stark River where it flows into Great Slave Lake in the Northwest Territories at Frontier Fishing Lodge. I had fly fished as a child, and then given it up for many years as I muddled my way through marriage, children, college, graduate school, a couple of transcontinental moves, divorce, and career. My skills were decidedly rusty. I was grateful to the pretty Arctic grayling that rose so eagerly to my clumsy casts. They were not spooked by less-than-perfect presentations, as trout so often are. And with the grayling's kind encouragement and steady practice, I got better. Arctic grayling grow to exceptional size in those chilly waters, and I caught some that were three to four pounds (1.3 to 1.8 kg), though the standard is more on the order of one or two (0.4 or 0.9 kg).

Because they are a comparatively small fish in a country where other sport species come in sizes marked large, giant, and humongous, Arctic grayling don't get the credit they deserve. They are delightful sport, fun to fish for because they hit fast, leap beautifully, and fight well. They are often underrated because they take easily, and because they are usually fished on tackle that is much too heavy. They should be fished on the lightest tackle possible—anything over

two-pound (0.9-kg) test is cheating. The real challenge with grayling
is not in luring them, but landing them. They have a tender mouth
and must be played carefully, especially when they are giving the
dazzled angler a series of spectacular leaps. This is a fish that takes
skill, not strength.

They are also exquisitely beautiful. They have been described by
one whose prose is more florid than mine as "the flower of fishes."
Their dark blue back fades into pale lavender on the sides, and to
top it off they have a dramatic dorsal fin that is charcoal grey with
violet and blue spots and topped with a bright red border. And the
final accolade: Arctic grayling is the most delicately flavored fish
ever created. Sautéed lightly in fresh butter with shallots and chant-
erelles, and Lucullus himself would beg for a dinner invitation.

Speaking of Kings

THE trouble with being an American fishing in Canada is that we
don't speak the same language. Take a perfectly simple thing like
salmon. A salmon's a salmon, right? Wrong. It's a king or a chinook,
a chum or a dog, unless you prefer color-coding, in which case you
have your choice of silver, pink, or red. And don't for a minute think
that Atlantic salmon are like any of the five species of Pacific salmon.
They're not.

Thoroughly baffled after a trip to Canada, I took my confusion
to Dr. John McCosker, director of Steinhardt Aquarium at the
California Academy of Sciences in San Francisco. With the aid of
his technical and authoritative *Dictionary of Fish*, we sorted it out.

Atlantic salmon (*Salmo salar*) are simply Atlantic salmon,
saumon Atlantique in French. That's easy enough. The West Coast
is a bit more complicated. The five Pacific species are all members
of the genus *Oncorhynchus*. *O. tschawytscha* is a chinook to Cana-

*King salmon is the choicest of the five
species of Pacific salmon.*

TOP: *Young king salmon range throughout the North Pacific from northern China to Alaska and down the West Coast to southern California. They feed on anchovies, rock cod, herring, squid, and larval crabs.*

MIDDLE: *Brook trout are fiesty little trout native to eastern North America. They were introduced to Europe and Argentina in 1884, and have been planted in cold streams throughout the United States.*

BOTTOM: *Sockeye salmon run up the Adams River in British Columbia to spawn. Salmon run upriver in both spring and autumn.*

dians, *un saumon royal* to the French Canadians, and a king or spring to Americans. *O. kisutch* is coho, silver, or *saumon argente*. *O. keta* is chum, dog, or keta salmon, unless it's *un saumon chien* or *saumon keta*. *O. gorbuscha* is the humpback, the pink, or *le saumon rose*. *O. nerka* is the sockeye, the red salmon, or *le saumon rouge*.

Then, of course, there are certain size distinctions to be made. Any fish over ten pounds (4.5 kg) is considered trophy-size. A chinook over twenty pounds (9 kg) is called a smiley; over thirty pounds (14 kg) it's a tyee. Anything bigger than that, be sure to get lots of pictures to show the grandchildren. Chinook average something under twenty pounds (9 kg), but that figure is skewed by the occasional monster in the sixty-to-one-hundred-pound (27 to 45 kg) range. Chum generally weigh seven to ten pounds (3 to 4.5 kg), silver and sockeye between five and eight pounds (2.3 to 3.6 kg) and humpbacks average between three and five pounds (1.4 to 2.3 kg).

© Chris Huss/Ellis Wildlife Collection

TOP: What Americans call spring or king salmon, is chinook to Canadians, le saumon royal *(royal salmon) to French Canadians. King salmon can weigh over 100 pounds (45 kg), but most average around 20 pounds (9 kg).*

BOTTOM: Salmon need clean, cold gravel-bottom streams like this one to spawn.

© Jeff Foott/Tom Stack & Associates

Where to Find the Fish and What to Call Them

TO find fish, you have to know where to look for them. Salmon are found on both the Atlantic and Pacific Coasts of the United States and Canada as well as the coasts of Europe. They are anadromous, fish that swim from the sea upstream to spawn in rivers. Their offspring then swim to the sea to mature, later returning to their home rivers to spawn themselves. Fish for them during the spring runs in rivers that flow into the ocean, in coastal waters in the summer, and in large landlocked lakes.

Trout live in cool-running streams, rivers, and lakes throughout the United States, Canada, and Europe. Like salmon, they prefer clean, gravelled streams. The chalk streams of southern England are the world's best-managed trout waters. There's decent brook trout fishing in New England wherever the fatal combination of too many fishermen and pollution have not killed them off. Colorado, Wyoming, Montana, and Idaho have some of the premier trout streams in the world, superb in the backcountry, under heavy pressure where roads make the fishing readily accessible. California, Oregon, Washington, and Alaska have excellent rainbow and steelhead fishing, though the best rainbow-trout fishing is undoubtedly found in Alaska.

Bass are found in streams, lakes, reservoirs, and ponds in all the lower forty-eight states and southern Canada as well. Smallmouth bass like deep pools and channels, rocks, and clean gravel. Largemouth bass may be found almost anywhere there's fresh water— farm ponds, shallow lakes, and slow streams. They prefer to hang out under floating logs, alongside stumps, and hidden under lily pads. Both smallmouth and largemouth bass (*Micropterus* sp.) are also known as black bass, and to confuse the issue further, neither is a true bass. They are both members of the sunfish family, as are rock bass, bluegills, and crappies.

© Francis & Donna Caldwell

OPPOSITE PAGE: One of those days when nothing exists except the still water, the crisp Colorado air, you, and the fish.

ABOVE: Smallmouth bass like this one are found in warm water all over the country.

True bass are white bass and yellow bass, but they usually get clumped under the heading of "panfish" along with bluegills, perch, and crappies. Panfish get their name from their convenient size: They fit just right in a frying pan, and they make a fine-tasting breakfast. They're also great fun because you can catch lots of them quickly. Best of all, you'll find them everywhere, for panfish are not terribly fussy about where they live.

Big bass feed at night—and this young angler has the proof.

© Wally Eberhart

They are often dismissed by haughty sports fishermen as a sort of "kindergarten" fish, but the fact is they've taught many an awkward beginner how to present a fly accurately, and how to fish a wet fly, since they usually feed under the surface. They also allow one to practice during the day, not being adverse to eating in hot, bright sun. A great many fish feed only in the early morning, late evening, and when the sky is heavily overcast (read: raining). These habits, I'm sure, were developed over time to protect them from their predators, including me, who would prefer not to be up at four in the morning in a damp dinghy, or holding up dinner trying to catch the evening rise, or huddled glumly in the rain in my foul-weather gear, hoping a big game fish will deign to dine with me.

It was from one of these so-called kindergarten fish, the yellow perch, that I learned the meaning of "nibble." My red-and-white bobber would dip, but my father would whisper, "Not yet." A moment later, the performance would be repeated, and again, my father would whisper, "Not yet." All of a sudden the bobber would disappear completely, and my father would say, "Now!" I usually set the hook and landed the fish all in one motion as I jerked the rod upward, flinging the fish back over my head onto the dock.

All the panfish swim in schools, the white perch in open water with a gravel bottom, the yellow perch among the weeds and snags in deep water, the crappies and bluegills in clear, shallow water in the shadow of stumps, sunken logs, and pilings. Panfish consider practically everything edible, from worms to wet flies to little silver spinners and spoons. A word to the wise: Some fish are easier to skin than to scale, and yellow perch are among them.

As with bass and trout, some of the fish called perch are not perch at all, and some fish that *are* true perch are called by different names entirely. Just for the record, white perch is actually related to the bass family, while the walleye, with the intimidating Latin name of *Stizostedion vitreum*, is a true perch. By the way, the yellow perch is one of those rare fish that's called a perch because, mirabile dictu, it is one.

BELOW: Yellow perch are most often found in cold water lakes in schools at depths of 20 to 30 feet (6 to 9 m). They weigh from ½ pound (.23 kg) to as much as 3 pounds (7.35 kg).

BOTTOM, LEFT: Black crappie like cold lakes, ponds, and slow-moving streams where they school in the water weeds. These were taken ice fishing.

BOTTOM: Here's the entree for an epicurean dinner—a fine, fat walleye. This fellow has reason to regret his trip from the bottom of the lake to the top.

BOTTOM, RIGHT: These Esox lucius *are known all over the northern United States and Canada by more than a dozen different common names: pike, great northern pike, Great Lakes pike, shovelnose pike, lake pickerel, jackpike, jack, snake, pickerel shark, gade, tosh, and luce. Pike like to lie in the weeds where they are perfectly camouflaged.*

OPPOSITE PAGE: There might be some good trout fishing in the pool below this waterfall in Glacier National Park in Montana.

Walleye are one of those species I described earlier that like to feed at inconvenient hours in inconvenient weather. Basically, they're night feeders, preferring darkness, which means they're caught most often on dark days, before dawn, or at twilight. I caught my first few walleye by accident: I was trolling deep with spinners and spoons for trophy-size lake trout. Since walleye school, as all perch do, where I caught one, I caught several. Now walleye aren't always great fighters, but to be brutally honest, neither are large lake trout. And while a walleye will never impress your friends and fellow-anglers the way a forty-pound (18-kg) lake trout will— they don't photograph as well—it is far better eating. I will cheer- fully release a big lake trout after I've gotten a quick photograph, but walleye I keep. As an epicure's delight, walleye ranks right up there with trout and salmon.

For pure sport, try pike. Great northern pike are not handsome; in fact, their looks are best described as eerily prehistoric. Found in northern Minnesota and Wisconsin, and north through Canada, they are tough, powerful fighters that hit hardware like a hot Ferrari. Every guide I've ever met hates them with a passion because they have razor-sharp, recurved teeth. While sticking your hand *in* to recover a lure that's in deep presents no particular problem, pulling your hand back *out* again does. Most Northern Country guides can show you impressive pike scars on their hands. Experienced anglers use heavy gloves to retrieve the hook. In addition, pike are extremely slippery and hard to handle, which doesn't make most folks like them any better.

The final blow is that they're lousy eating. I am not an anatomist, but the simple fact is that a pike has billions of bones, most of them the little, nasty kind. I've been told that pike can be rendered edible by soaking them in a spiced-brine-and-vinegar solution, but I'll bet it takes years to melt all those bones.

Still, northern pike are super sport. They take anything, take hard, and take serious exception to being boated, all of which make for exciting fishing. Since only the starving could consider them food, photograph the big ones, and send them back to their lair in the weeds to fight another day.

I once fished with a fellow on Lake Athabasca in Saskatchewan who hooked two very large pike. So proud was he of these great northern pike, that he decided not to photograph them, but to take them back to Lake Athabasca Lodge to claim his place as a man among men. The guide put the first one, a fine twenty-pounder (9-kg), on a metal stringer trailing over the side of the boat. The second one, even bigger, fought hard for fifteen minutes before it was brought to the boat. Just as the net was about to slide under it, the

pike gave one, last, mighty wrench, and *broke the steel leader in half.* To console himself for the loss of his biggest fish of the trip, the sorrowing fisherman reached for the stringer to gaze at his other pike, only to discover that it had *pulled apart the metal links of the stringer,* and escaped.

That's the end of the story about the pike, for they were never seen again. The fisherman drowned his sorrow in drink all afternoon and well into the night, and later claimed that the uncertain, weaving state of inebriation is the only proper manner in which to appropriately appreciate those uncertain, weaving curtains of light that are the aurora borealis.

When I was very little my father told me stories about muskies. His father had built a shingle cottage on Lake Tomahawk in Wisconsin in the Pottawatamie Colony, and there he had spent his childhood summers. When he grew a little older he became a camp counselor at the boys' camp on an island in the lake called Camp Minocqua. Over the fireplace in the camp's main lodge hung a huge stuffed muskellunge, taken, the boys were told solemnly, from that very lake. The first time I spent the summer at the cottage, my father fired up the old mahogany runabout and took me over expressly to show me that muskie.

I knew muskies were big; the one on the wall was bigger than I was. I knew they were fierce; they looked it. I knew they were cunning and wary; my father had told me how often he'd gone fishing

ABOVE: *Northern pike.*

BOTTOM: *Muskellunge.*

for muskie and come home skunked. I knew they haunted the weeds in the shallows, their camouflage colors concealing them perfectly in the shadows of sunken logs; my father had shown me the place where he'd hooked his. I knew they fought wildly; my father had told me many times how he'd hooked two, but never landed one.

I wanted to catch a muskie. Thank God, I never did. It would probably have yanked me into the water and had me for dinner. I still want to catch one, though. Muskies were not common then, and are less common now. I once read that the rarest fishing trophy in the world is to take a muskellunge on a fly. I would like to do that someday.

Millions upon millions of trout are produced in state fish hatcheries. The fry are planted in streams, rivers, and lakes. This is the state hatchery on Cape Cod in Sandwich, Massachusetts.

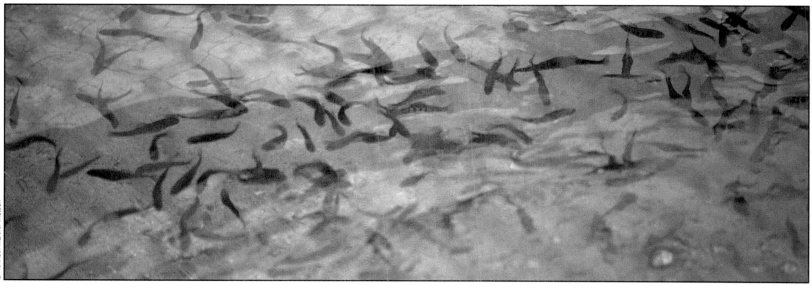

© Kenneth Martini/Amstock

Defining the Fish

WILDLIFE biologists divide fish into three categories. Natives are fish which have always been found in certain waters, such as rainbow trout in California's Sierra Nevada streams. Wild fish are species which were originally transplanted and then naturalized, such as black bass in the Potomac River. Catchables are fish raised in hatcheries and released by government agencies with the expectation that they will provide sport for that season, as they are not expected to survive to reproduce.

These swarming rainbow trout at the fish hatchery in Mammoth, California, represent but a miniscule percentage of the trout that will be released into California's streams and lakes. Rainbows tolerate warmer water than brown trout.

Stocking fish in streams and lakes grew, in part, out of the observation that there were fewer and fewer fish available each year. When the colonists first settled the eastern seaboard, Atlantic salmon swam up the streams in such numbers that farm laborers often refused to work unless promised that they would have to eat no more than one meal of salmon a week. In New York, masters were prohibited by law from requiring their servants to eat salmon more than once a day. Spawning Atlantic salmon were taken out of rivers with seine nets by the wagonload. (Atlantic salmon return to their home stream to spawn several times; the Pacific salmon spawns once and dies.) By the beginning of the nineteenth century, American writers were already bemoaning the shortage of fish in the streams, and the number of rivers rendered uninhabitable by dams and pollution. Barnwall, whose *Game Fishes of the North* is an American fishing classic, was among them. Published in 1862, *Game Fishes of the North* reported on the Atlantic salmon: "Hendrick Hudson, on ascending the river he discovered, was particularly struck with their immense numbers, and continually mentions 'great stores of salmon.' The last unhappy fish that was seen in the Hudson had his adventurous career terminated by the net, near Troy, in the year 1840."

As the pioneers marched west, the same story was repeated over and over. First, the cries of delight at the stunning abundance, and within a few years, cries of dismay at the declining numbers of all kinds of fish and game. Even today I see the same attitude in many parts of Alaska. 'It's the last frontier, the last place in the whole country where a man may live as he pleases, without wrestling daily with restrictions and rules and regulations; there's so much land, so many trees, so much game, so many fish, it'll last forever; there's always been more than plenty, and there always will be.' On the basis of such sophistry I've seen fishermen take ten times the fish they could eat for the sheer fun of it. Alaska still has a lot of fish by comparison with the lower forty-eight states, but that's not saying much. And the attitudes that have so devastated the fishing in the rest of the United States are all alive and well in Alaska.

Some people tried to do their own stocking, transporting eggs and fry in buckets from one stream or lake to another. Many species flourished; others upset the balance of nature, and the wild fish supplanted the natives.

Tilipia, a basslike fish from Africa, reproduces at an astonishing rate, a fact which led some people to think that it could be the answer to the problem of fewer fish and more fishermen. They guessed it might do well in certain American waters, and they were absolutely right: it did so well that no other fish could survive where there were tilipia. It is now illegal to plant tilipia in American waters.

The huge lake trout of the Great Lakes nearly succumbed to pollution, siltation, an infestation of lamprey eels, and the fishing pressure encouraged by a highway building program that made virtually every corner of the Great Lakes accessible. Huge cleanup programs are underway, and I hear that the fish are recovering. It's going to be a long haul; lake trout, like all cold water fish, grow

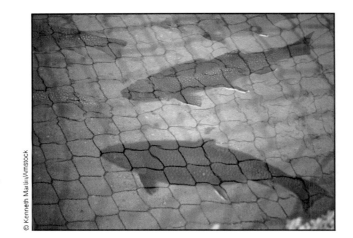

These hatchery-bred rainbows are protected by netting. It takes the eggs forty days to hatch, and it is estimated that 95 percent of the hatched fry are lost in the first three or four months. Rainbow trout are very nearly the perfect fish: They grow fast (6-7 pounds [2.7-3.1 kg] in three years); they take eagerly; they fight hard and well; and they are the next best thing to heaven when it comes to eating.

slowly, something on the order of an inch (25 mm) a year. The big lakers are still twenty-five years or more down the road.

Many state Fish and Game Departments run their own hatcheries, farming fish from eggs to fry, and dumping them by the millions into streams where they once flourished on their own. These are the catchables. I no longer fish in stocked streams because I find the fish poor sport even when they are as fine a species as rainbow trout. They haven't much fight in them, and they taste like the food they were fed at the hatchery. Not being intended to last more than a few months, they never have time to grow to any size to speak of. Besides, memorizing all the regulations about how many fish of so many inches (mm) may be taken on which days of the week makes going fishing less relaxing than sitting for the state bar exam. I prefer to fish light tackle and barbless hooks, catch-and-release only, and restrict my fishing to native fish who are willing to give me a serious argument about being caught.

FISHERMEN are like gardeners: wherever they go, they take the flowers—or fish—they love most and plant them. Many fish have flourished far from their native homes. The brown trout, indigenous to Germany, was imported to England from Germany, and in many places it is still called the German trout. From England and Germany it was planted in the streams of New York, and with the advent of the transcontinental railroads, to the Rocky Mountain streams of the Far West, the West Coast, and southern Canada.

Steelhead and coho salmon were planted in the Great Lakes, and eventually came to treat the Lakes like the ocean, running up

OPPOSITE PAGE: Good sport but not great eating, this great northern pike was taken on a spinning lure.

LEFT: Like the pike, the black crappie is found all over the country, and has a different alias everywhere it is found: calico bass, Oswego bass, strawberry bass, speckled bass, silver bass, lake bass, grass bass, sand perch, sun perch, spotted perch, calico bream, crapet calicot, and, of course, just plain crappie.

Wherever We Wander...

streams and rivers to spawn, and back to the Great Lakes to mature.

The rainbow trout traveled even farther. Not long after the turn of the century, Blaney Percival, one of the extraordinary characters of British East Africa, introduced the rainbow trout to Kenya where it was established by the mid-twenties, and it's still doing well. Taken from the West Coast of the United States to New Zealand, the rainbow has flourished, and often grows to sizes rarely found in its native haunts. Now Americans travel to New Zealand to fish for their own trout, and from all I'm told, it's fine fishing, too.

Early morning fly fishing from a canoe.

Bass are native to the St. Lawrence and Mississippi River basins and the southern Atlantic states. One enterprising nineteenth-century angler, William Shriver, decided the Potomac had everything one could reasonably expect of a river except black bass, and he personally took the responsibility for remedying that lack. Reports Brian Curtis in *The Life Story of the Fish*, "When the Baltimore and Ohio Railroad was completed across the Alleghenies, the event had one significance to Mr. Shriver: man had provided the link that nature had omitted. He procured a large bucket, punched it full of holes, and then hung it in the water tank of the locomotive while the train puffed down to the shores of the Potomac There he released his fish and there have been black bass in the Potomac ever since."

In 1879, 150 striped bass took the train from New Jersey to California where they were unceremoniously dumped in San Francisco Bay. A couple of years later a few more arrived, and stripers soon became one of the Bay's top game fish. Filling the Bay for building development (more than one-third of the Bay has been filled in the last century), water policies that severely reduce the amount of fresh water that flows into the Bay, and the impact of pollution,

Falling water aerates the river, which helps replenish the fishes' oxygen supply.

have all reduced stripers in both size and number, much to the dismay of Bay Area anglers. I used to hear stories from people who took their limit in two hours who now tell me they can't do it in two days.

Brook trout also made their way west, naturalizing beautifully in California's High Sierra streams, while rainbow trout swim happily in the streams of New England. Anglers on both sides of the continent can find streams with browns, brookies, rainbows, and cutthroats, each occupying its own little niche.

Welcome to the Thermocline

FRESHWATER fish live most comfortably in a fairly narrow temperature range from about 39° to about 70°F (3.9° to 21°C). Think of your local lake as a torte in three layers. The top layer is warmest, ranging from 75°F (24°C) at the surface to 70°F (21°C) at the bottom, and extends from the surface approximately fifteen feet (4.5 m)

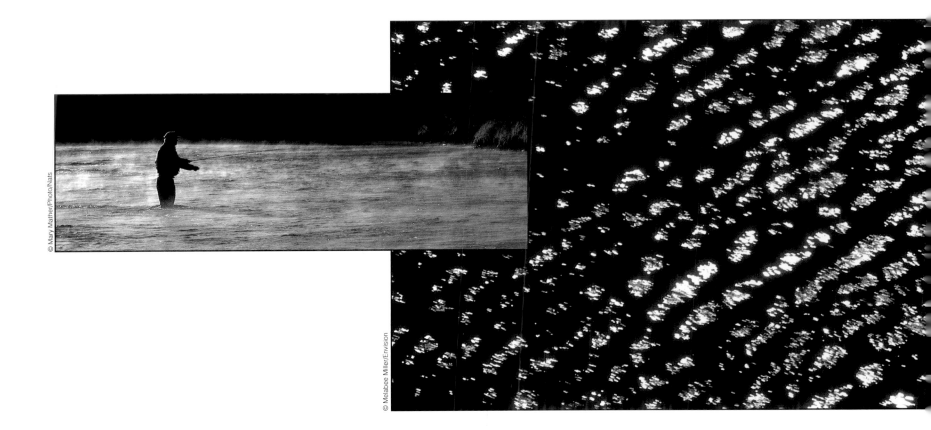

© Mary Mather/PhotoNats

© Melabee Miller/Envision

down. This layer is called the epilimnion, and while it's refreshing for people to swim in, it's too warm for most fish, particularly for feeding.

The second layer is the thermocline, which ranges in temperature from a maximum of 70°F (21°C) at the top to a low of about 45°F (7°C) at the bottom, and may be from ten to forty feet (3 to 12 m) deep. *That's where all the fish are.* That's where the combination of temperature, food, and oxygen are best for the fish. That's where, fishing a good lake on a summer's day, you'll catch trout, salmon, lake trout, walleye, and smallmouth bass, depending on which species live in your lake.

Below the thermocline, to the bottom of the lake, is a third layer, the hypolimnion. The temperature drops to water's maximum density point at 39.5°F (4°C), too cold to be comfortable for most fish. Unless there are bottom-loving water weeds, there is also too little oxygen to sustain fish.

To catch fish, keep your line in the thermocline.

Successful freshwater fishing depends upon keeping your line in the thermocline.

CHAPTER THREE

All the Fish in the Sea

Back

in the days when the

Santa Monica Pier still existed,

on the southern California

Coast, before the pounding

waves and wild winds

of the great

Pacific storms battered it to

pieces, my father

would take me fishing off the

pier. Saltwater fishing

was a casual operation in those

days. I didn't know what

I was fishing for,

© Peter Dombrovskis/Envision

Even if no fish bite, it's perfectly possible to spend the day watching the patterns of light on the water shift and change. What wonderful secrets lie below this calm surface, the secrets of all the fish in the sea . . .

and as long as it was willing to take my bait, I didn't care. The bait shop sold shiners, which were easy to put on the hook, and the man behind the counter spoke knowledgeably of what fish were biting and how the changing tide would affect the fishing. I listened to every word without understanding any of it.

The old men who lined the pier in silence let me look in their buckets to see what they'd caught, but they said little to me and less to their neighbors. What I did understand was that each fisherman had his secrets, some special, hard-won knowledge of which bait to use or how to cut it or how to put it on the hook or how to jig the line or where to cast. I knew, too, that fishermen never told their secrets. I would have to fish and fish for years until I learned my own secrets.

My father must have known some secrets, too, because we always came home with fish.

Saltwater fishing has an air of adventure about it that freshwater fishing doesn't quite share. Oceangoing fish are typically bigger and meatier, firmer fleshed, and harder fighting, than freshwater fish. There are more species to fish for, more and heavier tackle to choose from, and always, the ineluctable element of surprise. One never knows for certain what may take the bait. There are so many more fish in the sea.

© David Csepo/Ellis Wildlife Collection

King of the Seas

IT may be no more than local prejudice, but I think salmon are the finest fish that swim. The Pacific Coast has a lot of salmon, some five different species, and I've fished for a lot of salmon. But that's not the only reason I think so. Rare indeed is the refusal when I offer to share some of the Alaskan salmon I've caught. Rare, too, are the times that I see salmon offered at a reasonable price at the fish market. Last year, fishing a week at Whaler's Cove Lodge in Angoon, Alaska, I spent less on the whole trip, airfare and all, than if I'd bought the same amount of salmon at the store as I caught. That's without factoring in the fun of the fishing.

The prize of the Pacific, a king salmon. King salmon migrate more than 2,400 miles (3,840 km) out to sea from the mouth of their home river. They find their way back to spawn by the smell of their home waters.

Catching Pacific salmon on their spawning run seems to be largely a matter of annoying them sufficiently: Salmon don't feed running upstream. The fact that they do sometimes take a fly or a lure is generally attributed to their sense of territoriality, of feeling their space is being violated, causing them to strike out of pure pique. Salmon *do* feed in the ocean, and the best salmon fishing I've had has been trolling the coastal waters of Alaska and British Columbia.

A salmon often gives notice before taking. It taps the bait with its tail, just as it does to cripple a herring preparatory to making a meal of it. That slap makes the rod tip dip noticeably. Then it strikes. A good strike can bend the rod into an arc that would do credit to a rainbow.

An argument with a salmon follows a predictable course. It begins with the salmon making a hard run in the opposite direction while the angler worries that it'll run out the line to the backing. Then it makes a hard run back toward the boat, slackening the line and convincing the terrified angler that he's lost the fish entirely. Some fast cranking tightens up the line enough to raise the hope that the fish is still on. Hope leaps to conviction as the fish sounds, taking line out and nullifying most of the last five minutes worth of reeling.

Suddenly the salmon shakes its head violently, trying to throw the lure. Now the angler is certain the fish is gone for good, for another run toward the boat makes the line go nearly limp. Steady reeling and pumping brings the line taut once more, and the angler begins to think he may yet have a chance. As he gains steadily he prays that if he can't land it, God, could he just see it, please? It's fought so hard and it feels so big, if he could just see it, even if only for a moment.

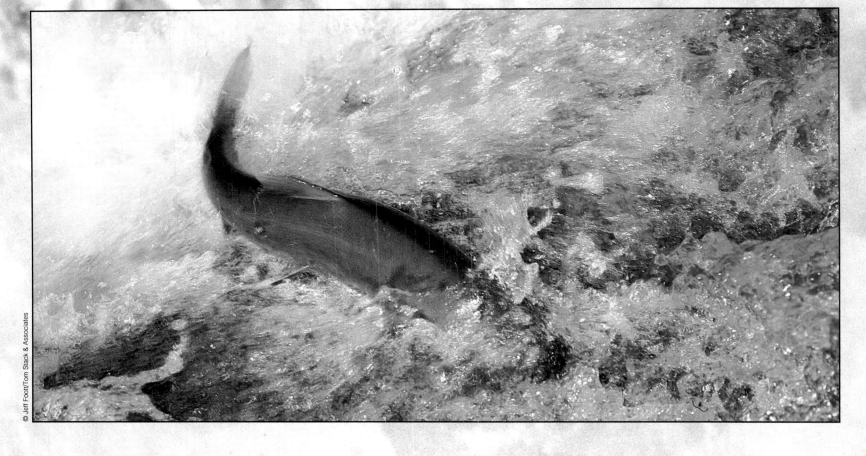

As if in answer to the unspoken prayer, the salmon leaps clear, its silver scales shining in the sun. In a flash of terrible self-knowl- edge, an angler's epiphany, the fisherman knows his prayer was the wickedest of lies: having seen it, he must have it. He bends to the task with a will, pitting his desire against the tiring fish. It leaps again and then once more, but the line thickens inexorably on the reel. At the sight of the boat, the fish shakes his head and tears off line in a desperate run. The angler tries to steady himself, for the moment of truth is near. A good hand with the net stands by as, rod high, line tight, the angler leads the fish again to the side. A swift scoop, and the salmon, bigger and more beautiful than he had dared dream, lays in the bottom of the boat, gleaming and perfect.

"A big tyee," the guide yells. The angler hesitates only an instant. "Let me get a picture, then let it go," he says. No sooner said than done. The guide skillfully removes the hook, and gently slips the silver king back into the dark waters. "How big do you think it was?" the angler wonders aloud. "Over thirty pounds (13.5 kg), easy."

It was a good fight with a good fish, a sporting contest between gentlemen, and now each goes his own way, having played well, having behaved honorably.

THIS PAGE: Most people know salmon swim upstream against the current, miles from the ocean to spawn. Few know that its Latin name, Salmo, means "the leaper"; this is because the salmon literally jump their way up waterfalls. These sockeye are returning to their spawning grounds in the Brooks River, past Brooks Falls, in Katmai National Park, Alaska.

INSET: Pacific sockeye salmon running up the Fish Way in Hell's Canyon, Fraser River, British Columbia.

Hauling Halibut

FISHING for halibut is so entirely different from fishing for salmon that it seems scarcely credible that both activities should be identified under the same rubric. It is a signal failure of language, a statement of its inadequacy, that both activities should be called fishing. Some other term must be found that describes the experience more accurately.

Allow me to explain the essential differences. Halibut do not look like fish. Once, in the misty past beyond the bounds of evolutionary time, they may have looked like a fish, but now they do not bear the faintest resemblance to the sleek, streamlined, powerful, silver shape that is a fighting fish. They look like something that was run over by a streamroller.

ABOVE AND OPPOSITE PAGE, TOP: California halibut average 50 pounds (22.5 kg), unlike their much heftier cousins, Pacific halibut.

Halibut do not swim. They lay on the bottom, flat as a flounder. They may allow themselves to drift now and then, but they do not swim, as anyone who has ever seen a salmon running free would use the word.

Halibut do not strike the bait. They may yawn and be snagged, perhaps, but they do not strike.

Halibut do not fight. They do not shake their heads. They do not have heads to shake. Fishing for halibut has all the adrenalin-rush, all the heart-pounding excitement, of reeling in a wet mattress.

Fishing for halibut is hard work. Halibut get big, very big. Three hundred pounds (135 kg) is not even close to record size. Imagine, if you will, the exhilarating fun of snagging a three-hundred-pound (135-kg) sodden mattress from the bottom of the ocean, reeling it to the surface, and dragging it into the boat.

It takes some serious work to boat a halibut, even a little one. In southeastern Alaska most of the boat captains automatically release any halibut under thirty pounds (13.5 kg). Imagine now the kick you'd get out of hauling something the size of an upholstered footstool from the depths of the sea, your arms aching, sweat dripping in your eyes, seventy-five or a hundred feet (23 to 30 m) straight up, only to have the captain tell you to put it back.

Halibut are flat stupid. They don't know how to be proper fish. A sensible fish fights all the way to the boat and goes wild when it finally sees the boat. Halibut just lay there like a log. Until you get them on board. Then they remember the part about fighting. They flop wildly. No fish club made will stun a halibut the first time it's applied. At this point, everyone aboard is cordially invited to do the halibut highstep, a popular Alaskan dance in which the lucky angler attempts to entangle every other person on board with the line while the captain attempts to stun the madly flopping fish with the club as the other parties aboard attempt to dodge the angler, the line, the fish, the club, and the captain simultaneously. Tradition requires that the halibut highstep be performed on a tossing boat deck treacherous with water and slime.

I once watched a small halibut bring an ex-Marine damn near to his knees. We were fishing with him and his youngest son, a sturdy, strapping lad of twenty or so. The father had just hauled up a halibut that weighed in at well under fifty pounds (23 kg), a job that had taken him the better part of thirty minutes. A high school

For big game fishing the angler is strapped into a fighting chair with a four-inch (10-cm) wide leather belt to prevent both from being hauled overboard.

© John Hutchinson/Envision

Pacific halibut lay on the ocean floor at depths anywhere from 20 to 1600 fathoms (165 to 13,200 feet or 50 to 4,000 m). That's a long way to haul a halibut before it breaks the surface.

football coach, he was in pretty good shape. Still, he laughingly admitted, his shoulders and arms were killing him. Too casually, he inquired as to whether it were possible to get a massage back at the lodge that evening. He watched his boy straining to haul in a halibut no bigger than the one he had caught.

He stretched his arms, wriggled his wrists, did a few kneebends, baited his hook again, and dropped it to the bottom. Standing behind him, I could hear a faint murmuring. Edging closer, I heard him talking to the halibut. He was muttering, "Please don't take my hook, please don't take my hook, please don't take my hook." And I understand perfectly. No man wishes to be shamed before his son.

Halibut have three redeeming features. They are easy to catch: You can take your limit, both fish, in less than an hour. They can be very big: Halibut to six hundred pounds (270 kg) are not common, but they are not unknown, either. They are excellent eating: One big halibut probably constitutes a lifetime supply of fine fillets. Given an electric winch with which to drag them up and a pitchfork with which to hold them down, I'd say it's definitely worth doing, though I'd hesitate to classify it as sport.

For these reasons, it seems likely that fishermen are going to continue to fish for halibut, and that being the case, I reiterate my plea for a new term that more accurately describes the experience. Bottom-snagging, perhaps. Or dredging. Or halibut hauling. But don't call it fishing.

LEFT: The largest known concentration of nesting bald eagles is in southeastern Alaska in and around the Tongass National Forest. Bald eagles are excellent at catching fish—one reason why so many breed along the Alaska coast where both food and shelter are available.

To Whistle Up Eagles

SOMETIMES life blesses us with felicitous coincidences. Not many years ago, I was offered the opportunity to spend two months in Africa. I walked away from a comfortable corporate career in San Francisco, preferring to slog through the Okavango Delta with the chief of a local T'swana tribe and the British Ambassador to Botswana, among others. Having made our way nearly eighty miles (128 km) through the reeds, water lilies, leeches, crocodiles, and hippos in dugout canoes, we arrived wet and weary at the Kerr-Downey-Selby camp at Mambo. Tony Henley, one of the last of the big game hunters of Africa, materialized out of the trees to take us to camp, and give us hot showers, hot tea, and a magnificent dinner. More importantly, he offered to take me fishing in the morning.

Fishing by itself is plenty of reason to get up eagerly in the morning, but Tony had offered another blandishment. He was going to call an eagle so that I could photograph it diving for the fish. We found a wide place in the river to park the boat, cut the engine, and dropped our lines to the bottom for catfish. Tony said we wanted them about three or four pounds (1.4 or 1.8 kg). It didn't take long

BELOW: This African fish eagle has stooped to the kill, its wings spread to brake, talons ready to grab a fish that has strayed perilously close to the surface.

CENTER: Hippos feed at night on land and rest underwater during the day, surfacing now and then to breathe.

to collect several. It took even less time to get the boat out of there when a massive hippo came snuffling to the surface about five yards (4.5 m) off our bow, its little pig eyes calculating and baleful. We didn't wait to see how long it would take it to reach us; hippos have a nasty habit of barreling boats over and consuming their contents.

Safely out of the hippo's reach, we cut a handful of hollow reeds and stuffed them deep into the fish's mouth to make it float. Then Tony held the fish in the air and whistled. Two African fish eagles rose into the sky and landed on trees bordering the water, eyeing the fish in the same interested manner that the hippo had considered us. Tony gave me a count to set the motor drive on the camera, gave the fish a mighty heave, and my film recorded a series of blurs as one of the eagles rose, stooped powerfully, screaming all the way, and snatched the fish as it hit the water. We did it twice more, and the

© F. S. Mitchell/Tom Stack & Associates

last time *I* called the eagle with the four part whistle that signals the eagle's dive for the kill. It was one of the most exciting things I'd ever done, to whistle up an eagle.

Three days after returning to the United States from Africa, I went up to British Columbia for some trophy salmon fishing at North Pacific Springs Lodge. We had a good morning's fishing, taking several handsome king salmon, when my fishing partner, Russ, offered me a special treat, so special, in fact, that he wouldn't tell me what it was. All he would say, looking smugly pleased with himself, was that I couldn't have it unless I caught some rockfish for him. Now rockfish are not considered particularly choice eating where king and silver salmon are available, so I didn't think he was going to have the cook prepare some gourmet treat. Still, I was game. I caught him four or five profoundly ugly rockfish.

Bald eagles tear their fish into bite-size shreds with their sharp, hooked beaks. Within a few minutes there's nothing left but bones.

A Meditation on the Tapestry of the Universe

The guide gunned the boat off to a beautiful little cove where he landed Russ, a tripod, and his Leica-*cum*-600-mm lens. The guide took me back to the entrance of the cove. Russ gave the signal that he was ready to shoot. Suddenly the guide tossed one of the rockfish as high in the air as he could throw it, and gave the same whistling cry of the eagle I'd learned in Africa. Instantly a bald eagle rose, stooped, and snatched it right out of the air. I grabbed the next fish, called the eagle with the cry for the kill, and threw the fish far out onto the water. Another eagle took it in a mighty splash. Russ's photo shows that eagle rising out of sundazzled spray on mighty wings, the rockfish tight in its talons.

A year or so later I gave a slide show at a huge convention hall on the best places in the world to fish. I showed the photos of the African fish eagle and the American bald eagle, and then I gave that heartstopping cry. Behind me I heard a little girl ask her father, "How does she do that?" I turned around and whispered, "Come up after, and I'll show you." Thank heavens she had been properly reared: The child already knew how to whistle. In five minutes she'd mastered it, and someday I hope she gets a chance to whistle up an eagle.

THE old paradigm of the universe was that we could only come to understanding by breaking down its immensity into small digestible pieces. Thus biology was separated from physics, physics from geology, geology from botany. The smaller the bite we took, the more honored we became: the specialist always garnered more prestige, always achieved higher position, and the ultimate accolade, was always paid more.

Now a new paradigm is emerging. We seek to gather up all the

tiny pieces of the puzzle into which we have fractured and splintered the universe, and are attempting to fit it back together again. We are seeking to see, not how things differ, but how they interrelate. We wish to look at the tapestry instead of at the threads and knots.

By this circuitous course I come to the relationship between birds and fish. A wise fisherman finds fish by watching the sky. Big fish eat little fish. Often a school of good game fish, like tuna, will chase smaller fish to the surface. Depending on where one is in the world, seagulls, frigate birds, terns, and other seabirds will feed on the baitfish driven to the surface, congregating and diving in great, wheeling flocks. The fisherman who spots the birds knows where the big fish are. They're right below the little fish.

Flocks of feeding birds mark schools of fish. Herring gulls like large baitfish. Terns indicate bluefish, mackerel, and striped bass. Gannets mark mackerel. Shearwaters, fulmars, frigate (man-of-war) birds, and petrels feed over tuna. Pelicans diving in tropical waters are a sure sign of mullet.

Trophy Bluefin Tuna

Bluefin tuna are superb sport, renowned for their tremendous strength, speed, and hard fight. They range all over the world from cool temperate waters to subtropical seas.

TUNA are members of the mackerel family and good game fish. They come in several varieties, depending on where in the world one fishes: bluefin, yellowfin, blackfin, yellow tail, big-eye tuna, and albacore. They are heavy-bodied and hard-fighting.

In the form of the giant bluefin tuna, they are also an extraordinary trophy. For reasons no one has pegged completely, something unusual happens to bluefin tuna when they migrate as far north as Nova Scotia and New Brunswick. The bluefin that migrate from the Caribbean to the eastern seaboard are excellent sport, but they are not in the same class with the giant tuna that feed in Canada's northern waters. The giant bluefin tuna caught off St. George's Banks and in the Canso Strait commonly go to over one thousand pounds (450 kg). The world record bluefin tuna, caught in the Canso Strait between Nova Scotia and Cape Breton Island, weighed in at 1,496 pounds (673 kg).

Just to give you some basis for comparison, that's approximately fifteen times bigger than I am. When I received an invitation to go fish for one of these monsters, instead of doing the sensible thing and crawling under the bed until the danger was past, I accepted at once. Advised to bring my heavy clothes for November in Nova Scotia, I packed a bag so heavy it practically gave the Boeing 767 a hernia. There were wool watch caps, thermal underwear, cotton turtlenecks, flannel shirts, Irish fisherman's knit sweaters, goose-down parkas, wool socks with silk liners, thick gloves, all topped off with foul weather gear. I include this list so that you may plan your trip to Nova Scotia in November to catch the giant bluefin tuna more wisely than I: it wasn't enough to keep me warm.

One makes an interesting arrangement with the captain one hires. For the cost of his hire, he trolls you through likely waters from seven in the morning until six at night, or until you freeze to

Tuna fishing in Nova Scotia.

A school of Bluefin tuna.

© Francis & Donna Caldwell

Deep-sea fishing calls for heavy tackle, good leverage, and a fighting chair securely bolted to the deck to ensure that the angler stays on the boat.

death, whichever comes first. The boat is fully equipped with a fighting chair into which the victim is firmly strapped with a leather belt four inches (10 cm) wide, just in case he tries to make a break and run for it after a fish is on. The captain provides all the necessary tackle, and I will confess honestly, I had never seen such huge Penn reels in my life. I'll bet when they're finished using those reels for trophy bluefin tuna, they rig them to towtrucks and use them to haul cars out of ditches. The boats are fine, sturdy vessels and I'm reasonably sure that one of those tuna would have to work hard to haul the boat stern-first to certain death at the bottom of the sea, though I'm not fool enough to suggest it couldn't be done.

Should you actually catch one of these monsters, the fish is the captain's; all you paid for was the frostbite and the fight.

That's probably a blessing though, since even a small one, say, a thousand pounds (450 kg), is probably sufficient unto the thousandth generation, and you would have to go to your grave knowing that no one in your family would ever forgive you for making them eat nothing but tuna casserole for the rest of their lives.

Fortunately, we were spared this dreadful fate. We trolled the waters of Canso Strait from morning till night in rough water without ever getting into fish. Reports over the marine radio suggested they were feeding off St. George's Banks and had not yet made their way down to the Strait. It was blowing hard over choppy seas that day, and the next morning a storm came up so severe that we were forced to forego our second day of fishing.

We spent the day exploring Cape Breton Island, poking in antique shops where I found wonderful hand-carved, hand-painted, articulated wooden lures of the sort that are called 'collectible' and sell for terrifying prices where I live. There were antique rods and reels and wicker fishing creels and a monogrammed silver fly box that could be attached to a belt. There were hand-carved wooden duck decoys, which I bought, and a set of fine china fish plates with leaping trout on them that I did not, and I regret that decision still. We had high tea in an old Scottish inn called the Inverness and watched the rain lash the mullioned windows while we swallowed scalding tea and feasted on scones and jam and biscuits and slices of a fancy cake covered with Chantilly cream. Our guide showed us all the trout streams that are good fishing come spring.

We did not catch any trophy bluefin tuna, it is true, but I know they're out there, and one of these days I'll go back to Nova Scotia and try again. And next time I'll dress warmly.

The Seductive Fly

*F*ly fishing

is an elegant sport.

For many men it is seductive,

as a charming woman is

seductive. When the besotted

fellow tries to remember

what it was that a woman said

that was so charming,

he often pulls up short

against the realization,

that it was not so much what

she said, as what she listened to

with such intelligent interest

and understanding.

Courtesy Orvis Company, Inc.

SO it is with fly fishing: it is the way an exquisitely balanced rod is built, the way it feels, the way it responds, that is so irresistably enticing.

But that is only fly casting from the outside, the way it appears to the fascinated eye. To try the trick oneself is as complicated and contrary as coming to know a complex woman. The rod will not obey. The line will not lay long and lovely on the water. The fly will not drop delicately upon the surface, nor will it go where it was willed to go.

For the beginners all manners of madness beset the enterprise. The hook catches hats and coats and trees and rocks with equal impartiality. The line lays in squiggles on the pool. The act of casting throws one magnificently off balance, demonstrating in an unmistakable way precisely how slippery wet rocks can be. It is learning by the seat-of-the-pants, and the seat of the pants is often wet.

There are dozens of books on proper casting technique, and every one proposes something different. Not that it matters; it is impossible to learn to fly cast from the written word anyway. One may pick up hints, one may take encouragement, one may find some mnemonic device that jars the arm into a form somewhat closer to the correct one, but no one can read a book and learn to cast a line.

The only way to learn is to watch someone who is very, very good, and then prevail upon them to teach you how. But how does the mere novice determine who is very, very good? First, the rod must mark an arc no more than a quarter-circle on the sky. The finest description of how to fly cast is in Norman MacLean's great classic, *A River Runs Through It*: "It is an art that is performed on a four-count rhythm between ten and two o'clock, and closer to twelve than to two." Next, the line must lift lightly from the water

© Francis & Donna Caldwell

OPPOSITE PAGE: Native to Europe, North Africa, and western Asia, the brown trout was introduced to the United States in 1883.

TOP, LEFT: The dry fly, such as this visible beetle fly, invented by Frederick Halford in England in 1886, was adopted and adapted by Theodore Gordon to American streams at the turn of the twentieth century. Gordon's flies were designed to match species of insects native to North America, rather than England.

ABOVE: Cutthroats were first identified in 1806. With siltation from lumbering, pollution, the introduction of other species that competed with them for food, and the fact that they are not easy to raise in hatcheries, it was feared that they would become extinct before the end of the twentieth century. Crossbreeding inland cutthroats with sea-run cutthroats in the 1960s did bring the population back somewhat. This angler found good cutthroat fishing in Cayuse Creek, Idaho.

Dry flies like these from Orvis are dressed with floatant so they'll float on the water. They are intended to look as much as possible like an insect that fell into the water. When there are real insects dropping into the water, the angler's challenge is to "match the hatch" as closely as possible.

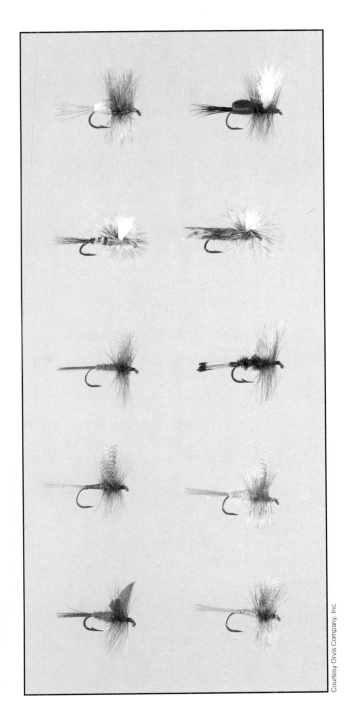

and carve a graceful curve of backcast behind the tip of the rod. At the precise instant that the backcast comes straight, the forward cast must begin, dropping fly, leader, and line, in that order, upon the water. That in itself is a tall order, as any beginner who has tried it can affirm. But there is more. The fly must be presented not only delicately, not only naturally, but accurately. It must drop, not on the trout's nose, but above it and very slightly to one side, for trout, unless rising, take to the side.

MacLean, who learned to cast from his father, wrote that, "If our father had had his say, nobody who did not know how to fish would be allowed to disgrace a fish by catching him." MacLean goes on to explain, "Until man is redeemed he will always take a fly rod too far back. Then, since it is natural for man to try to attain power without recovering grace, he whips the line back and forth making it whistle each way, and sometimes even snapping off the fly from the leader, but the power that was going to transport the little fly across the river somehow gets diverted into building a bird's nest of line, leader, and fly that falls out of the air into the water about ten feet (3 m) in front of the fisherman."

MacLean was not the first to observe that fly casting must be an art, because it most assuredly is not a science. Washington Irving, fresh from reading Izaak Walton's *The Compleat Angler*, found himself inspired to give the sport a whirl. "For my part, I was always a bungler at all kinds of sport that required either patience or adroitness, and had not angled above half an hour before I had "satisfied the sentiment," and convinced myself of Izaak Walton's opinion, that angling is something like poetry—a man must be born to it. I hooked myself instead of the fish; tangled my line in every tree; lost my bait; broke my rod; until I gave up the attempt in despair…"

There are some combinations of the student-teacher relationship

that seem particularly happy for learning to fly cast. Grandparent

to grandchild is one, father to child another. Husband to wife is not.

A friend and avid fly fisherman, a man I hold in high regard and

warm affection, eager to share the joys of fly fishing with his wife

who had recently presented him with a darling daughter, special-

ordered made-to-measure waders, the finest money could buy, to

celebrate her first Mother's Day. His colleagues, knowing well how

he loved his wife and wishing only to preserve him in his joy, sent

around a petition, signed by every soul who worked in the office,

pointing out that such an act probably constituted grounds for

divorce. Bowing to pressure, he did purchase something more

suitable to give her, along with the waders. A card, I believe.

Friend-to-friend may also serve the purpose well, but barring

these three, a stranger or acquaintance may work best. When I

decided to take up fly fishing for the first time since childhood, I

spent my lunch hours perusing the tackle available in the fishing

department at Eddie Bauer. The manager of the department was a

member of the Golden Gate Angler's Club and the world champion

tournament fly caster. I asked advice about equipment; he gave it

generously. I questioned him closely on technique; he demonstrated

This is classic trout water. The most famous trout streams of the United States include Henry's Fork of the Snake River, the Madison, the Gallatin, the Roaring Fork, and the Firehold in the West, the Au Sable in Michigan and the Battenkill in Vermont. In Canada, the Babine and Okanagan rivers in British Columbia and the Bow River in Alberta are superb fishing.

TOP: With waders, a hat, and a water-proof jacket it's possible to have some very fine fishing and never get wet. As my father always said, "Fish like rain."

BOTTOM: Here is everything you need to fly fish: a fly rod, a single action reel, flies and fly box, and a landing net.

in the middle of the store. I wanted to know where to go for the best fly fishing; he invited me to attend the Thursday lunchtime lectures and slide shows that went on through the spring.

He showed me the casting pools on the roof at Eddie Bauer's, built for gentlemen from the San Francisco Financial District to test rods on when the building had housed the venerable Abercrombie & Fitch. When I finally made the arrangements for my first big fishing trip and purchased my first good outfit, he offered to meet me at the casting pools in Golden Gate Park at seven in the morning on several consecutive Saturdays to teach me himself.

I remember well the hours spent before the casting pools trying to throw my thumb at the sky while simultaneously keeping my elbow back. The mist rose slowly off the water, the foghorns groaned outside the Golden Gate, a great blue heron beat its way toward the sea. I gripped the rod with such intensity that the stripped-out line left red marks on my fingers.

When my lesson was over, and I was left to practice what I'd learned, the members of the Golden Gate Casting Club who had been watching the proceedings with some curiosity, kept me on track. They watched my backcast straighten and told me when to begin the forward cast, so I could get the rhythm. They told me when my rod was too far back and when, overcompensating, I did not take it back far enough. They tossed on the pools little yellow rings of the sort used for playing horseshoes and told me to put my fly in the center of it. When I finally succeeded, they moved them farther from me, teaching me to lengthen my cast by degrees. They explained what wind knots were and how to cut them off and replace the leader. They sat at the table in the clubhouse that looks out on the pools and taught me the knots that link leader to line and fly to leader. And while they taught, they told me stories of the fish they'd caught over long lifetimes of fishing, stories of salmon that used to spawn in San Francisco creeks, stories of steelhead big enough and tough enough to snap a twenty-pound (9-kg) test line. I longed to catch such a fish, and I knew that when I did, I must not disgrace the fish, myself, or these men.

LOGIC would suggest that acquiring a good fishing outfit would be fairly simple. It isn't. Logic would further suggest that this acquisition should involve only a modest expenditure. Logic is wrong once again. Logic, as you may have already begun to suspect, has nothing whatsoever to do with fishing, not the fish, not the fisherman, and most assuredly, not the tackle.

Essentially, fishing demands nothing but some string, a stick to tie to one end, and a hook to tie to the other. Why is it, then, that every angler I have ever known departs for a fishing trip, whether

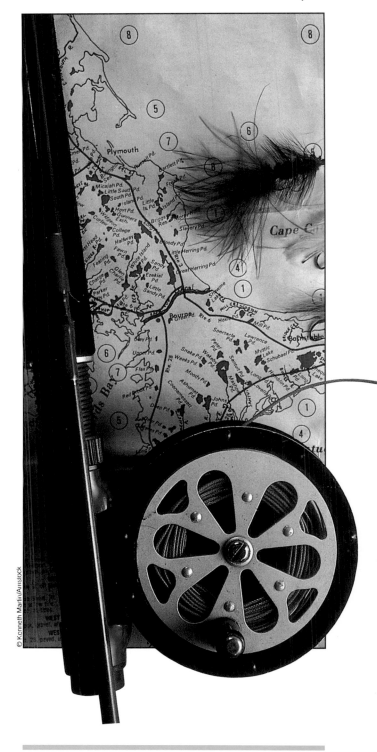

This is the stuff of winter dreams and summer delights: fly tackle and a map of the streams to fish come the next vacation.

Getting the Gear

Courtesy Orvis Company, Inc.

Courtesy Orvis Company, Inc.

for a day or a week, with enough gear to furnish the entire inventory of a well-stocked tackle store? On one recent occasion my outfit included a fiberglass fly rod, a breakdown fly rod to fit in my daypack, a custom-made graphite fly rod, a spin-casting rod, three fly reels, two spinning reels, dry flies, wet flies, floating lines, sinking lines, extra leaders, spare hooks, Mepps and Rapala lures, a cloth to clean my lines, floatant to float the flies, nail clippers to clip leaders, clear nail polish to seal knots, surgical forceps to remove hooks, and a stringer, just in case I caught something. This is merely the tackle. It does not include such essentials as polarized sunglasses, a Swiss Army knife, and Muskol (a 100 percent DEET insect repellant, which, by the way, will melt both sunglasses frames and fishing line). Nor does it include the foul weather gear, in case it rains, or the Panama hat, in case it doesn't. I haven't even mentioned the split shot for sinkers and the pliers to put them on with, but I'm sure you take my point. I have often contemplated the profound and troubling philosophical question of whether or not the hardest part of fishing is assembling the tackle.

The Rod, the Reel, and the Line

I have not, in fact, even touched upon the true complexity of the business of selecting tackle. Purists believe the best rods are made of split bamboo, and reject the newer materials as a form of heresy. An invocation of the merits of Tonkin cane (*Arundinaria amabilis*) is a sacred litany among anglers who cherish the classic. The finest

American rods were produced by rodmakers like Hiram Leonard and E.F. Payne in the East, and E.C. Powell in the West, around the turn of the century, and they are today rare, expensive, and much sought after by collectors. A contemporary rod of tea stick bamboo (Tonkin cane) will today set an angler back well over a thousand U.S. dollars.

Still and all, the truth is, almost no one fishes with the great old rods; they are retired to a place of honor on the wall of the library where one can savor the sight of them as one does the taste of a fine cognac. They are sufficiently valuable that few anglers are willing to risk breaking them by fishing them. It was true then and it is true today, that rod tips are fragile, and the best rods always came and still do, with two rod tips for that very reason.

There are other considerations as well. The old rod guides were built for the silk lines of the day and are far too narrow to accept the width of modern lines. And that's before one gets into the issues of antique solid-plate reels that require removing all one's line and hanging it out to dry after each day's fishing.

Fiberglass supplanted bamboo, and there are still plenty of fiberglass rods to be found, but it has been itself supplanted by exotic laminates of space-age materials adapted from the aerospace industry, such as graphite. Graphite is astonishingly flexible, able to endure almost any strain, able to bend nearly in half without breaking. It is also brittle, and a sharp blow may shatter it, the sort of impact that could, for example, accompany the discovery by the angler of an unexpectedly slippery rock or an unanticipated hole.

Most graphite rods are laminated combinations of fiberglass and graphite. They are extremely light, weighing anywhere from one and three-eighths ounces to three ounces (39 to 84 g). Graphite has the lovely ability to make me a better caster than I am.

OPPOSITE PAGE, TOP: A western rod like this one from Orvis has a more flexible tip, which gives the line greater speed and allows longer casts, especially when it's windy.

OPPOSITE PAGE, BOTTOM: These Orvis reels are good sturdy reels. Devout anglers dream of owning Hardy Perfect reels or custom-made Bogdan reels someday.

© Betty Groskin

ABOVE: Tying one's own flies is one of the pleasures of fly fishing. These are streamer flies, tied during a long winter spent anticipating the coming spring's fishing.

BELOW: Today floating and sinking plastic fly lines have replaced the silk lines of the last century, and the twisted or braided horsehair lines used three hundred years ago.

Courtesy Orvis Company, Inc.

The rod, the reel, and a good brook trout—
all that's required for a perfect day of fishing.

Courtesy Orvis Company, Inc.

ABOVE: Modern rods are usually 8 or 9 feet (2.4 or 2.7 m) long and 15 feet (4.5 m) at most; the seventeenth-century angler hefted fir and whalebone rods 20 feet (6 m) long.

I own a graphite rod built by the late Ferd Claudio of San Francisco that I consider magical. Fishing once at Wollaston Lake Lodge in northern Saskatchewan, the guide watched me make a series of casts that, properly ranked, ranged from the merely awkward to the impossible. I was absolutely honest; I gave full credit to the rod. After about a half-hour of this, he asked if he might try it and we traded rods. It took me another half-hour to persuade him to give it back. I had some genuine doubts about whether I'd ever get my hands on it again. I could see the guide calculating how much bigger he was than I am, and mulling over how serious an investigation the Mounties would make of a drowned American angler.

The real state-of-the-art in fly rods at the moment is graphite/boron rods. Proponents claim they have the power to throw the line for long casts or in the wind as well as the same felicity for accuracy that graphite rods have.

Having disposed neatly of the question of rods, there is next the reel. Reels have two functions: they hold the line and they retrieve it. Beyond that, everything is "features." Most modern fly reels are perforated on the sides to dry line quickly. On many reels, it is possible to change drag settings, spools of line, and the handle from right-hand to left-hand, though not, of course, while playing a fish. Most reels are made of aluminum or aluminum alloys, and those for saltwater fishing are treated with finishes that help prevent corrosion. Some reels are multiplying reels, which means that they are geared to pull in more than one rotation's worth of line per crank so you can retrieve line faster. A lot of the features sound more useful than they are, but only experience can teach which ones are worthwhile to you. The now-departed, much-lamented Sheridan Andreas Mulholland Anderson, fly fisher *par excellence*, recommended the single-action reel in his invaluable comic book of fly fishing, *The*

Curtis Creek Manifesto, for these reasons: It's simpler; it has greater line capacity; it's easier to maintain; it's lighter; it has a wider range of use; it builds character. What more could one honestly ask of a reel?

One of the great clichés of fishing writing is the one about "the line singing off the reel," but I never realized until I perused the Orvis catalog that reels are specially *designed* to sing. Allow me to quote the description of their Battenkill® reels: "We take great pleasure in the sound of our reels, and we've provided an audible drag in both the line-out and line-in directions—but you can change the drag in the line-out direction to silent with a flip of your finger."

The best tackle shops will allow you to rig a rod and take it out to the parking lot to test, which also gives you a way to determine how your reel will sing, though only on line-out, there being so few fish that thrive in parking lots.

Rods and reels are pretty straightforward. The reel holds the line, the rod throws the line. That's not too complicated. Lines are a ball of snakes by comparison. Lines are tied to leaders which are tied to tippets which are tied to flies at the business end. At the opposite end, lines are connected to backing which is either tied or spliced with epoxy to the line and wrapped on the reel spool. That's the easy part.

The hard part is to figure out whether you need floating or sinking lines, and if sinking lines, whether the whole line should sink or only the tip. Sinking lines are rated from slow (1 to 1½ inches or 25 to 37.5 mm per second) to fast (3½ to 5½ inches or 87.5 to 137.5 mm per second), with some in between. Floating lines come with options like double tapers, forward-floating tapers, front loops, and fluorescent colors for those who fish in the dark or nearly dark. The rational way to determine what is required for the particular sort of

Courtesy Orvis Company, Inc.

TOP: These D-XR reels by Orvis have a disc-drag to help keep the line taut when a fish is on, and are made of anodized aluminum, stainless steel, and naval bronze to resist saltwater corrosion.

BOTTOM: Modern reels fasten to the butt end of the rod. In past centuries the reel was attached one-third of the way up the rod.

© Francis & Donna Caldwell

And Now the Fly

fishing you propose to do is to find a good tackle shop, confess everything, and throw yourself at the mercy of the proprietor.

IF it seems there are a bewildering plethora of rods and reels and lines to bewilder and benumb the mind of the fly fisherman, they are as nothing when compared to the types and numbers of flies. Fortunately, that fact works in your favor. Because it's virtually impossible to know all of the 25,000-odd flies made, hardly anyone does. It is considered good form to ask local anglers, tackle shop owners, and guides which flies do best on a given piece of water under the specific circumstances you intend to fish it. I give you my word of honor as a Girl Scout ten years in uniform that the fly shops at Henry's Fork of the Snake River, on the Battenkill, or on the Au Sable will know exactly which flies take best on their river.

That said, there are some basics. Flies are divided into some broad categories, specifically dry flies, wet flies, and nymphs. Dry flies typically have upright wings or stiff hair (hackle) that stands straight up. They are usually, though not always, fished floating on the surface at the speed of the current with no drag from the line to betray them. A tiny dab of water-repellant mucilin or floatant helps keep them on top of the water. The theory behind dry flies is that they look like a live winged creature to a fish, often the *ephemera*, those clouds of minute bugs that live but a day and die. Those clouds of bugs are called a 'hatch' and tying on a fly that approximates the appearance of whatever it is that happens to be swarming about at the moment is called 'matching the hatch.'

Wet flies are usually, though not always, fished below the surface of the water. They resemble nothing known to people, though they may look to a fish like drowned bugs with wings that point over the

1.

2.

3.

4.

back. The action similar to a struggling bug is what really draws the fish. Wet flys are the traditional method of fishing for Atlantic salmon with the fly cast across the stream and dragged across the current.

Nymphs are supposed to resemble the larvae of aquatic insects. They do not have wings, and look mostly brown or gray and fuzzy. They are usually, but not always, fished underwater. Nymphs are a fairly recent development in fly fishing, the twentieth century's most dramatic innovation of technique and style. Nymphs dead drift, floating free with the current as a larva broken loose from the bottom would. There can be no drag from the line to spoil the effect of being carried by the current.

TOP: A collection of taking flies: (1) Woolly Worm; (2) Giant Black Stonefly; (3) Hendrickson Wet; and (4) Black Gnat Wet.

BOTTOM: Nymphs imitate larval stages of various insects as well as some crustaceans; dry flies imitate the adult stages. Streamers and bucktails don't imitate insects at all; they're supposed to look like minnows.

In general, one can get away with saying that flies that are intended to resemble natural insects are called 'imitator' patterns. The flies that resemble nothing natural are called 'attractor' patterns. Unfortunately, it is difficult to determine sometimes whether one is to look at these things from the angler's point of view or the fish's. Imitators, theoretically, put the fish in mind of terrestrial insects like beetles, bees, wasps, grasshoppers, locusts, spiders, moths, and ants, or stream-bred insects like mayflies, stoneflies, and caddisflies. Attractors theoretically arouse the fish's curiosity or threaten its sense of territoriality. For example, Black Woolly Buggers don't look like anything in nature, but spawning salmon will hit the damn things with a vengeance when they won't touch anything else. One knowledgeable fly fisherman tried to wiggle out of the debate of imitators vs. attractors by venturing that wet flies look a little like everything, and nothing like anything specific, which theory may end the debate, but does not answer the angler's burning question, "Why does the fish take the fly?"

Current theory declares that trout take flies based on size, shape, and color. Then, since that doesn't really explain it all, action is thrown in, and the *coup de grace* is delivered by the notion of territoriality, which states that big fish will go after anything that invades their feeding territory, pretty much no matter what it looks like.

In the end, after all the learned discourse, one is left with a little evidence, a lot of theories, and no proof. Why any particular fish takes any particular fly on any particular day under any particular conditions is as profound a mystery as how many angels can comfortably disport themselves on the head of a pin. Some days, the fish bite; some days, they don't. Beyond that, no one can speak with certainty.

Hooked on Lies

HACKLE and herl, hurled at the sky,

lays upon the water, a dead lie,

luring the lunker from its lie.

A sidelong swirl betrays the act,

one dark lie abandoned for another.

Lies anglers tell are told trout first,

and should the trout unwittingly, unwarily,

swallow the lie,

the same lie will be told, times without number,

to other trout and other men.

Dame Juliana Berners

ABOVE: A pole, a line, a hook, a stream, a fish, and an angler: that's where the sport of fishing began more than five hundred years ago. This woodcut is from Dame Juliana Berners' The Treatise of Fishing with an Angle.

WHO'D have thought a fifteenth-century nun could cause a riot that lasted over five hundred years? The only verified facts are these: Dame Juliana Berners wrote a versification of the terms of venery on hunting sometime before 1450. Terms of venery are those like *school* of fish, *pod* of whales, and *flock* of birds; the term for the group is determined by the specific animal in question. Such knowledge was considered an essential part of a young knight's education during the age of chivalry. The hunting treatise was printed in the *Book of St. Albans*. In 1496, the second *Book of St. Albans* appeared, this time including an essay titled *The Treatise of Fishing with an Angle*. Dame Juliana's name appeared on both editions; no man's name did. And that's what caused the riot.

With Henry VIII's destruction of the monasteries, the libraries were destroyed as well. Unfortunately, monasteries had most of the books in England; private collections were rare in a country where the vast majority of the population could not read. Only one copy of the manuscript version, copies by a scribe about 1450, is still known to exist. It is now in the Yale library, the gift of David Wagstaff, the late American angling collector. With the monastery libraries went most of the church records as well. Beyond her name and her book, nothing more is known of Dame Juliana.

That did not stop antiquarians from inventing a fascinating legend about her. In 1559, a century after the lady herself, John Bale described her, on the basis of no evidence at all, as an illustrious female, "said to have edited a small work on Fishing." While it is true that many books of that period were compilations of previously written poems and essays, there is no other known work on the sport of fishing, and to reduce Dame Juliana from the author to an editor is a cruel cut. Holinshed's *Chronicles* endowed her with noble rank in 1577, and by 1611 she had so improved herself that John Pits described her as not only noble, but a manlike woman. William Burton (1575–1645) scribbled some notes in his copy of the *Book of St. Albans*, claiming that the book was written by Lady Juliana Berners, of the locally noted Berners family, that she was Lady Prioress of Sopwell, and that the book was printed in the Abbey of St. Albans. All of which is most intriguing, but entirely unsupported by any evidence or documentation.

Antiquarians of the eighteenth and nineteenth centuries specifically denied the possibility that Dame Juliana Berners could have written *The Treatise of Fishing*. They fretted at length over whether it was possible that a woman might be both a sportswoman and nun.

In a facsimile edition of the second *Book of St. Albans* (1810), Joseph Halewood resolved the controversy neatly by proposing that she had been first one and then the other, a young noblewoman given to hunting, who, disappointed in love, retired to a convent. But he still denied her credit for *The Treatise of Fishing*.

He was already too late. Dame Juliana Berners was saved from drowning in centuries of speculation by Izaak Walton. In 1760 the eighth edition of Walton's *The Compleat Angler* was reprinted (the original appeared in 1653) with an introduction by one John Hawkins who credited Dame Juliana as the author of *The Treatise of Fishing*, taking the issue out of the hands of the antiquarians and placing it firmly in the hearts of fishermen. Any angler who reads the essay knows instinctively that the writer fished often and well— and there is no other name on either the manuscript or the books than that of Dame Juliana.

Why is *The Treatise of Fishing with an Angle* important? It was, "a remarkable event in the history of fishing," declares John McDonald in *The Origins of Angling*. Written in the early fifteenth century—Dame Juliana was probably born in 1388—it is an original work in an age when most writing was a revision of earlier material. There is virtually no writing on the subject of fishing as a sport prior to Dame Juliana's delightful essay. Her description of fishing dominated the angling world for the two hundred years following its publication. If the popularity of the eighth edition of *The Compleat Angler* rescued her name from anonymity, Walton did no more than pay the debt he owed her, for his book drew heavily on hers. To quote McDonald once again, "As the sole progenitor of the literature of the sport, [*The Treatise of Fishing with an Angle*] thereafter formed the main line of angling tradition. It remains one of the best essays ever written on the sport."

For baits for large fishes, adhere especially to this rule, namely, when you have caught a large fish, open its stomach and use what you will find within as bait, for it is the best possible bait.

***Dame Juliana Berners*,**
The Treatise of Fishing with an Angle,
first published as Book of St. Albans, 1496.

To Match the Hatch

DAME JULIANA knew that various insects appear according to the season, knew that fish eat them in their season, and knew that the angler whose fly closely approximated the hatch would catch fish. In fact, she gave such precise instructions on how to tie her flies, one for each month of the year, that the Angler's Club of New York displays a set of this venerable dozen tied by Dr. William Coleman.

Izaak Walton followed Dame Juliana's sterling example; in *The Compleat Angler*, Piscator told the honest Venator how to make a dozen artificial flies and when to use each one.

A big brown trout shatters the surface.

© Wally Eberhart

"You are to note, that there are twelve kinds of artificially made flies to angle with on top of the water. Note, by the way, that the fittest season of using these is in a blustering windy day, when the waters are so troubled that the natural fly cannot be seen, or rest upon them. The first is the dun-fly in March: the body is made of dun wool; the wings, of the partridge's feathers. The second is another dun-fly: the body of black wool; and the wings made of the black drake's feathers, and of the feathers under his tail. The third is the stone-fly, in April: the body is made of black wool; made yellow

These flies are replicas of some of the flies Dame Juliana Berners discussed in The Treatise of Fishing with an Angle.

TOP TO BOTTOM, COLUMN 1: March Brown, Dark Hendrickson, Royal Coachman, March Brown Emerger Parachute. COLUMN 2: Dark Elk Hair Caddis, Light Elk Hair Caddis, Adams. COLUMN 3: Green Paradrake, Quill Gordon, Olive Elk Caddis, Olive Thorax.

under the wings and under the tail, and so made with the wings of the drake. The fourth is the ruddy-fly, in the beginning of May: the body made of red wool, wrapt about with black silk; and the feathers are the wings of the drake, with the wings of the red capon also, which hang dangling on his sides next to the tail. The fifth is the yellow or greenish fly (in May likewise): the body made of yellow wool: and the wings made of the red cock's hackle or tail. The sixth is the black-fly, in May also: the body made of black wool, and lapped about with the herle of a peacock's tail; the wings are made of the wings of a brown capon, with his blue feathers in his head. The seventh is the sad yellow-fly, in June: the body is made of black wool, with a yellow list on either side; and the wings taken off the wings of a buzzard, bound with black braked hemp. The eighth is the moorish-fly: made with the body of duskish wool: and the wings made of the blackish mail of the drake. The ninth is the tawny-fly, good until the middle of June: the body made of tawny wool, the wings made contrary, one against the other, made of the whitish mail of the white drake. The tenth is the wasp-fly, in July: the body made of black wool, lapped about with yellow silk; the wings made of the feathers of the drake, or of the buzzard. The eleventh is the shell fly, good in mid-July: the body made of greenish wool, lapped about with the herle of a peacock's tail, and the wings made of the wings of the buzzard. The twelfth is the dark drake-fly, good in August: the body made with black wool, lapped about with black silk; his wings are made with the mail of the black drake, with a black head. Thus have you a jury of flies, likely to betray and condemn all the trouts in the river."

Curious anglers will find in their fly boxes flies that come very close to matching those that Dame Juliana recommended five hundred years ago. The fish and the *Ephemera* remain the same.

To Tie the Fly

Courtesy Orvis Company, Inc.

Winter is for tying flies; summer is for fishing them. Perhaps Gerard Manley Hopkins, the Victorian poet, put it best when he referred to the essentials of fly tying as "gear and tackle and trim."

IN Britain, Dame Juliana was the first to write of angling as a sport; then Izaak Walton expanded on the subject. In America, Mary Orvis classified the flies used all over the United States and Canada; then Theodore Gordon developed dry flies specifically for American waters. Orvis' book. *Favorite Flies and Their Histories* (1892), contained thirty-two color plates of 290 flies then in use which helped standardize patterns and their names. It also contained letters from fly fishermen all over the continent who described their favorite flies and which flies took best on their home waters, making the book an invaluable guide to anglers fishing streams or rivers new to them. Herself a brilliant fly tier, Orvis single-handedly made the Orvis name famous for its superb flies. The adverb 'single-handedly,' is doubly accurate: Mary Orvis tied without a vise.

Orvis' book clarified which flies were most effective in American waters; at the same time Gordon was working on a new area, the

Courtesy Eppinger

development of dry flies designed to match American hatches. Until the *fin de siecle*, all flies were wet flies based on British patterns, tied with soft hackles, wings that sloped back, and absorbent materials that sank quickly. They were fished downstream, under water.

Gordon tried stiff-hackled, delicate designs on the lightest hooks he could find. His goal was to imitate the insects found in the Northern Hemisphere, but he realized that no combination of feathers, fur, wool, silk, and steel could match the fragility and delicacy of the natural. "The more I study the imitation of the natural fly and the various books on the subject (or which treat of it)," Gordon wrote in the *Fishing Gazette*, "the surer I am that the trout have a wonderful eye for color but a very indifferent notion of form. There is any quantity of evidence; but take your mayfly alone and note the curious buzzards that are mistaken for the natural, particularly hackle patterns that are deadly because so nearly right in color."

On the Question of Color

THEODORE GORDON's conclusion that the key to a successful fly is its color brought him full circle back to the earliest known writings on fishing. In Book XV of *De Animalium Naturum*, written about A.D. 200, Claudius Aelian reported, "[The Macedonian fishermen] have planned a snare for the fish, and get the better of them by their fishermen's craft. They fasten red (crimson red) wool round a hook, and fit on to the wool two feathers which grew under a cock's wattles, and which in color are like wax. Then they throw their snare, and the fish, attracted and maddened by the color, comes up, thinking to get a dainty mouthful; when, however, it opens its jaws, it is caught by the hook and enjoys a bitter repast, a captive."

Dame Juliana knew the same thing. "In the beginning of May a good fly, the body of ruddy wool and lapped about with black silk; the wings of the drake of the red capon's hackle," was the fly of choice she informed the hopeful fifteenth-century angler. Izaak Walton, perhaps borrowing from Dame Juliana, told the fly fishermen of the mid-seventeeth century, "The fourth is the ruddy-fly, in the beginning of May: the body is made of red wool wrapt about with black silk; and the feathers are the wings of the drake, with the feathers of the red capon also, which hang dangling on his sides next to the trail."

Mary Orvis called this fly the Red Hackle in 1892. Today Orvis stores sell a similar soft-hackle fly as the Tup's Indispensible. It still catches fish, just as it did nearly two thousand years ago.

FISH hide. They hide around rocks, logs, under banks, and in weeds. Fish feed. They feed downstream from riffles and at the mouths of streams where they enter lakes. Fish rest. They rest in back-eddies and in the heads and tails of large, deep pools. Looking for the ripples that indicate a large obstruction just below the surface or watching the current to spot the quiet eddies is called 'reading the water.' Sailors do it to see where the next gust of wind is coming from before it hits the sail or where the reef is before it hits the keel; anglers do it to figure out where the fish are.

Fish usually face upstream to let the current bring the food to them. Big-feeding fish frequent slicks, smooth places where there are breaks in the current. Fish also lie in pockets, depressions in the bottom of streams, especially in riffles. They rest behind rocks and logs and in eddies so they don't have to fight the current all the time.

BELOW: One of England's classic chalk streams, the River Isis in Oxford.

Reading the Water

© Tim Gibson/Envision

TOP: It looks as though a low-water fly is what's called for in this fast-running glacial stream.

BOTTOM: Trout hold out of the current, facing upstream, waiting for food to come to them. Where in this photograph would you want to present your fly?

A Matter of Style

The serenity of England's lovely chalk streams is evident here at Lichfield Cathedral, Lichfield, England.

IT'S important to point out that all the description given thus far of fly fishing is only a description of American fly fishing. It is done differently in Britain. The British angler rents a private beat along one of England's lovely, quiet chalk streams, and for that day or week, may be one of only two or three people fishing that particular stretch of water. The British only cast to a rising fish, or more accurately, to a rising trout. The classic description is that Americans fish the water, the British fish the fish. That difference developed from the fact the streams of the two countries are not at all the same. American streams tend to be faster running in wilder country where it's rare to see a fish except during the evening rise. Britain's clear streams flow gently through grassy meadows where it's comparatively simple to walk along the bank and spot individual fish.

The British angler often works with a ghillie who rigs the rod, suggests the fly, points out the rising fish, recommends the strategy, handles the gaff or landing net, and kills the fish. The angler's job is to make the strike and play the fish; he need never touch it. Good creels and big fish are often displayed in the evening at the hotel. All fish are entered in the fishing register so one can see from day to day, week to week, year to year, how the fishing's been on any beat.

The best water on the famous chalk streams—the Test, the Itchen, the Dart—is private, but it is still entirely possible to obtain day or week tickets along a hotel's private beat, or less expensively, on the town waters. The prime fishing beats of the Test are largely owned by the very exclusive Houghten Club, but excellent fishing may be had along other Test beats and along the tributary streams.

British anglers dress the part differently from Americans. On the whole, their style tends to be a bit more formal than the lucky fishing cap, jeans, and T-shirts affected by American anglers. Part of the reason is that it's frequently too chilly for T-shirts; that, and the fact that the British think T-shirts are underwear. A turtleneck and a wool sweater are simply more comfortable, with or without the Harris tweed jacket with suede patches at the elbow. Tweed jackets and ascots are certainly not required, nor is a good briar pipe, but it probably wouldn't do serious harm to observe the local traditions.

Structure

PROFESSIONALS, or those who wish they were, like to talk about structure. Structure means anything that isn't water. It's whatever lies along the shoreline, anything that comes up from the bottom, like rocks and reefs, and anything that extends down to the bottom, like snags or pilings. Fish hang around structures because food is more abundant and the current is gentler.

TOP: A fly fisherwoman covers the water expertly on the Madison River, Yellowstone, Wyoming.

BOTTOM: This angler is gently removing the hook to release a trout back into Hat Creek, one of California's best trout streams.

The deeper clear water is, the darker it looks. The deeper the water, the harder to see the fish. Polarized sunglasses can help you spot fish; the thing to look for is movement and fish shadows on the bottom. Color isn't much help because most fish are well camouflaged.

© Mary Mather/Photo/Nats

© David E. Rowley/Envision

In lakes, expect to find fish at inlets and coves, along weedy shorelines or flats, just off points, and in weedbeds. Springs bubbling up from the lake bottom or flowing into a lake have a constant temperature range from 45° to 55°F (7° to 13°C) that attracts fish. Fish also congregate near the bottoms of deep channels and off submerged ledges and reefs. When it's windy, fish swim at the surface on the upwind side, beneath the surface on the downwind side.

FISHING is like birding or botanizing, one of those splendid passions that goes with one wherever one goes. I have birded, botanized, and fished in the Arctic and on the Equator, in the Yukon and the Northwest Territories, in the Sea of Cortez and on the shores on the Indian Ocean, in both the Pacific and the Atlantic Oceans, and in the Okavango Delta, where one of Africa's mighty rivers disappears into the sands of the Kalihari Desert instead of flowing out to sea.

Osa Johnson, a wildlife photographer who explored Africa in the 1920s and 1930s, was a serious angler who never passed up an opportunity to present the fish of British East Africa (Kenya) with a tempting fly. Of fishing the Gura River on her birthday, she writes:

"At dawn, I awoke and was off to try my luck at fishing. Martin [her husband, photographer Martin Johnson] was still asleep when I returned to camp with a 2½-pound [1-kg] brown trout. I was very proud and excited over the surprise I would give him for breakfast.

"But I was dripping wet, for I had fallen into a pool in trying to jump across, and it was so refreshing and cool that I had just lain there and soaked. I had slid down elephant trails and was covered with mud. My hair was moist and unkempt. My nails were dirty. And my boots were soaked and covered with goo. I was so wet that I just stood on my head and let the water run out of my boots. The fish was the only clean thing in the picture."

The story she told that convinced me to carry a pack rod wherever I go—I keep one in the car and one in my daypack whenever I travel—is this one:

"After several days we arrived at Nanyuki, and I settled down to fishing in earnest. That morning Martin drove me upstream into the pines and cedars. I planned to fish the stream back to camp.

"The river was stocked with the ova of brown and rainbow trout brought out from England. It was a major achievement on the part

Portable Passions

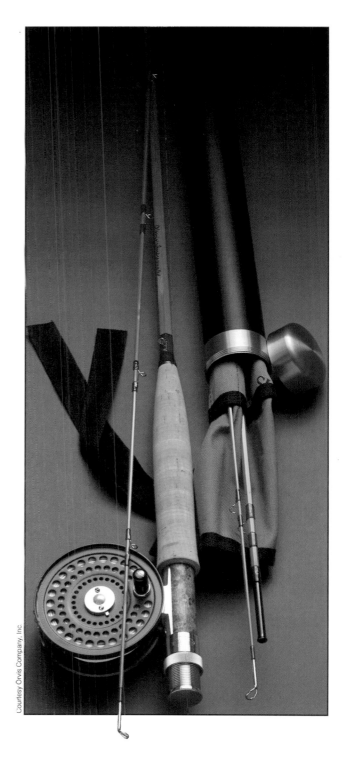

Courtesy Orvis Company, Inc.

Purists insist that nothing—not graphite, not graphite-boron, nothing—matches the delicacy and performance of a Tonkin cane bamboo fly rod. All Orvis tea-stick bamboo rods are registered by number, and they'll have your name put on yours, if you like.

of the government to import the ova from London, at terrific expense and 'shrinkage,' and send them in tins on the backs of porters over this vast area and up to altitudes of 11,000 and 12,000 feet [3,300 and 3,600 m] to deposit the eggs in streams. But the "dividends" have been millions of splendid fish and great pleasure for the settlers and visitors from abroad.

"The trout love gay-colored flys, for the insects of Africa are brilliant-hued. Most of the flies we use at home for salmon can be used in Africa for trout: The Durham Ranger, Silver Doctor, Jock Scott, Alexandra, all gave me great fishing, and I took my poundage [kg] records on number six hooks with a 3½-ounce [98-g] Hardy rod.

"The streams are crystal clear and cold, most of them tumbling down from high altitudes, the Mount Kenya streams coming directly from glaciers at the top. So I dyed my leaders green to make them invisible.

"Because rainbow trout are cannibals and because streams are so heavily stocked, the authorities encourage one to make large catches. I have caught fifteen from a single pool in one day and gone back the next day and taken as many from the same pool.

FROM LEFT TO RIGHT: The Black Dose and the Cosseboom, the Rusty Rat and the Undertaker, the Hairy Mary and the Silver Rat, the Black Bear Green Butt and the Blue Charm are some of the amusing names of flies.

"So well stocked is this river that on it I have caught sixty pounds [27 kg] of brown trout in a single morning, each weighing from a pound and a half to six pounds [.7 to 27 kg]. Sometimes, on drop flies, I have taken as many as three trout on a single cast, and I once took a total of one hundred and forty-eight trout in one day. Occasionally I would pick out one of the huge old cannibals of eight to ten pounds [3.6 to 4.5 kg].

"The streams are gloriously beautiful—the surrounding forest alive with sound and movement, the towering cedars festooned with creepers and Spanish moss, the vines flowering into whites and pinks and blues, orchids clinging to the branches, the sun and shadows making lively patterns on the stream, the birds calling and flashing color. Beneath giant fern trees grow all the ferns known to us at home, as well as many others. Vines make fantastic patterns, and I used to swing in them as I did when I was a little girl, and often found them useful to carry me across a stream in a tough spot.

"Gorgeous colobus monkeys swung about in trees, uttering their weird, low cries. They were among the most beautiful creatures of the jungle, with their long black and white brilliantined fur.

"Blue kingfishers with red beaks flashed through the sunlight and dived hungrily for little trout; black hornbill sounded their "anvils," and magnificently colored butterflies literally filled the air about me.

"There in the water, beneath the dipping leafy branch of a great tree, I would glimpse a trout, lazily loafing, his nose upstream, sometimes with others about him. One whip cast, dropping the fly under his nose, and the trout was mine."

This kind of trout fishing no longer exists anywhere on earth. So many fish were taken in the days before careful conservation that today what fish are left must be heavily protected. Perhaps the efforts made in conservation and stream restoration will someday allow this fabulous abundance to exist once more.

TOP: Brown trout look like salmon except for the fact that the angle of the jaw extends well behind the eye.

BOTTOM: Mt. Kenya.

CHAPTER FIVE

Spin Casting

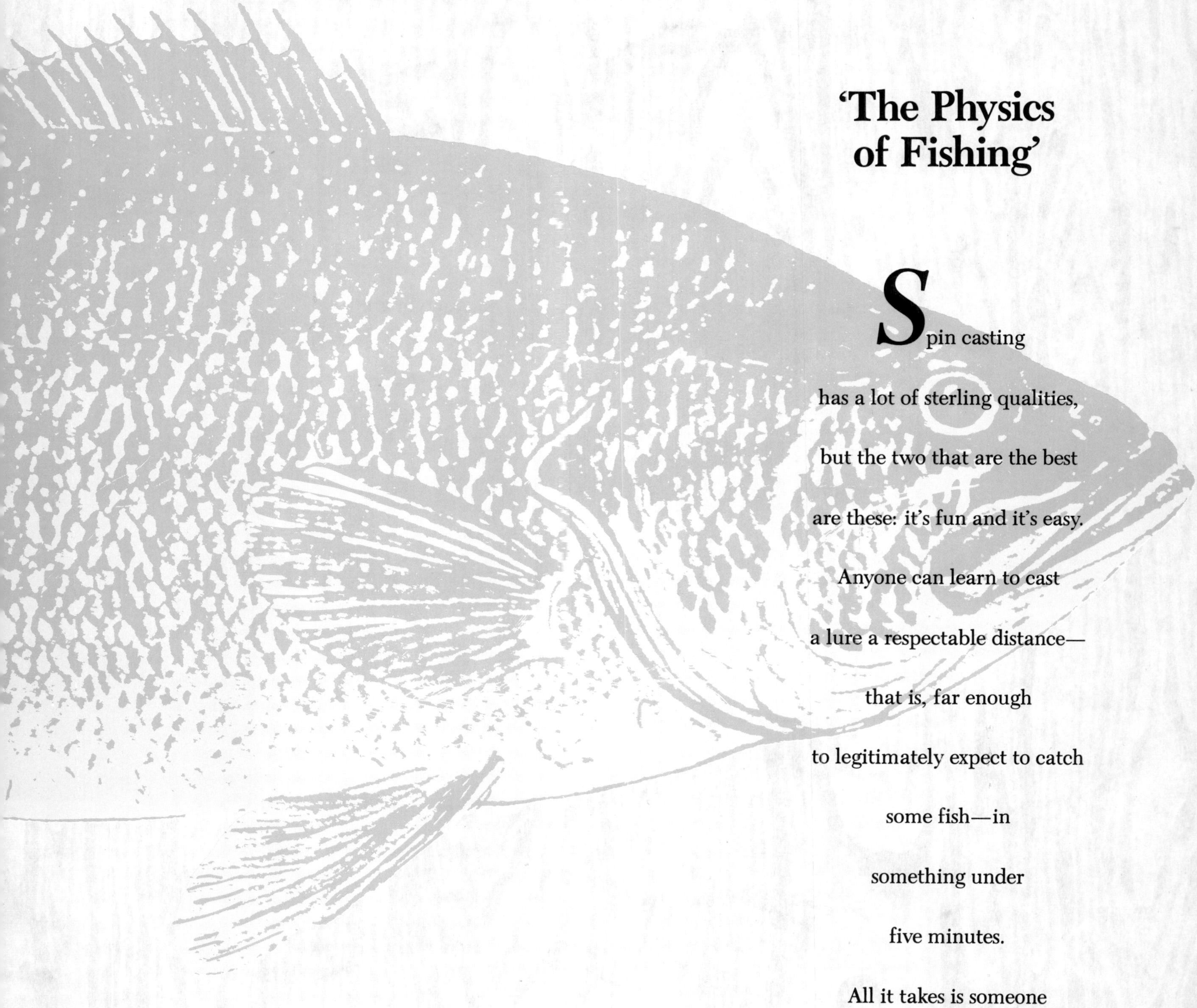

'The Physics of Fishing'

Spin casting has a lot of sterling qualities, but the two that are the best are these: it's fun and it's easy. Anyone can learn to cast a lure a respectable distance—that is, far enough to legitimately expect to catch some fish—in something under five minutes. All it takes is someone to show you how. But while it can be learned in a moment, it takes nothing less than twenty pages to describe the process. This curious fact reminds me of a quote from *The New York Times*, though the point of the *Times's* observation was somewhat different: "The Lord's Prayer contains 56 words, the Twenty-Third Psalm 118, the Gettysburg Address 226 words and the Ten Commandments 297 words. The U.S. Department of Agriculture directive on pricing cabbage weighs in at 15,629 words." I have no intention of getting into a contest of prolixity with the U.S.D.A., so instead I shall admonish you, dear reader, to find a friend who knows how to spin-cast, and watch. You'll have it down cold in five minutes or less.

Spin casting differs from fly casting in its application of the laws of physics. In spin casting, the weight of the lure carries the line; in fly fishing, the weight of the line carries the fly. That's because it's easier to throw something that has a bit of weight and mass to it than something that does not. If you found first-year physics baffling in the extreme you can demonstrate this principle by getting yourself a feather and a small rock. Throw the feather as far as you can. Then throw the rock as far as you can. Did it suddenly come clear? You have just demonstrated the laws of mass and velocity. In many ways, physics is a lot easier than learning how to outwit a fish, but since most people are convinced that physics is hard and fishing is fun, more people become fishermen than physicists. If the same people spent as much time at physics as they do at fishing, the country would be overrun with physicists instead of fishermen.

Spin casting is applied physics. The energy of your arm is transmitted through the rod to the line to the lure which flies, dragging the line behind it. Gravity pulls the lure toward the bottom of whatever body of water you happen to be fishing. When a fish bites, the energy of the strike (or the nibble) is transmitted through the lure to the line to the rod to your hand. See how simple it is? The concept

of transfer of energy is considered among the most difficult notions of physics to master, yet fishermen apply it every time they cast and catch a fish.

This proves one of two things: Physics isn't nearly as hard as most people think it is, or fishermen are smarter than physicists. I shall, at this point, withdraw, and allow you, gentle reader, to draw your own conclusions.

Surf fishing—a particularly pleasant way to spend a sunset on South Cape Beach, Mashpee, Massachusetts.

The Reel Thing

SPINNING reels are used for still fishing—leaning against a tree, feet propped up, reading a book; trolling—line trailing out behind a moving boat going slightly slower than the fish one hopes to catch; and casting. They hold and retrieve monofilament line. Terminology for the three basic types varies from America to Great Britain. What Americans call a spinning reel, the British call a fixed-spool reel; what Americans call a spin-casting reel, the British call a closed-face fixed-spool reel; and what Americans call a bait-casting reel, the British refer to as a multiplier reel.

On the spinning and bait-casting models, the line is visible on the spool; on the spinning reel the line on a spool is an enclosed housing. Common features are drags which make it harder for the fish to take out line, multiplier gears that let the angler retrieve line faster, level-wind mechanisms that keep the retrieved line evenly aligned on the spool, and anti-backlash features that prevent hours of muttering and swearing as you untangle a bird's nest of snarled line.

Ordinarily, the bigger the fish you're after, the bigger the reel you need to store sufficient line to hold the fish when it runs or sounds. Top-of-the-line reels are from Penn and Shimano. Penns are best known for their reliability and durability, Shimanos for their light, smooth action. Browning makes good medium-priced spinning reels.

Reels are attached to spinning rods which can run in length from six feet (1.8 m) for one-handed casting to 14 feet (4 m) for surf casting. Most spinning rods today are made of fiberglass or graphite, though every now and then an attic or basement yields up an old rod of good bamboo. The finest spinning rods are produced by Powell or Loomis. Good rods may be had from Fenwick, Kunan (whose founders came from Fenwick), Sage, and Browning.

Courtesy Cabela's

Spinning reels were originally designed for casting light baits. Today they are used primarily for still fishing and trolling.

Courtesy Daiwa Corporation

TOP: Spin-casting reels are fixed-spool reels, with the mechanism enclosed in a case. The line emerges from a small hole in the front of the reel.

BOTTOM: Bait-casting rods have an offset handle and reelseat to improve the accuracy of the cast; they come with multiplier gears, star drag, and a level-wind mechanism.

BELOW, RIGHT: Lead core line has an outer sheath of braided Dacron™ fibers which gives strength to the soft lead core inside. Lead core line sinks deep without using sinkers, thanks to the weight of the lead, but it has no elasticity.

THE vast majority of line used for fishing is monofilament, a single thread of extruded nylon. It is rated by the manufacturer according to the weight it can hold without breaking. A two-pound (0.9-kg) test line will hold up to two pounds (0.9 kg) without breaking. Most anglers choose their line on the basis of the size of the fish they're after. If the fish rarely gets over two pounds (0.9 kg), they'll use two-pound (0.9-kg) test and feel secure that the line won't break while they're fighting the fish. In the last few years a new sporting trend has struck the sport, fishing on light tackle.

Light tackle means using lighter rods and low-test lines. Light tackle has two advantages: it gives the fish a fighting chance, and it's more fun for the angler, requiring skill instead of strength. A three-pound (1.4-kg) bass on two-pound (0.9-kg) test line feels like a much larger fish. Using light tackle is also a greater challenge, requiring the angler to play the fish carefully to land it, since it could break the line at any moment.

Getting a Line on Line

As fine a catch of bluefish as anyone might hope to see. Bluefish are also called elf, skipjack, and tailor, and they travel in large schools. That means if you watch one, keep fishing; there are lots more out there. Bluefish can weigh up to 31 pounds (14 kg), but are usually between 10 and 15 pounds (4.5 and 6.8 kg).

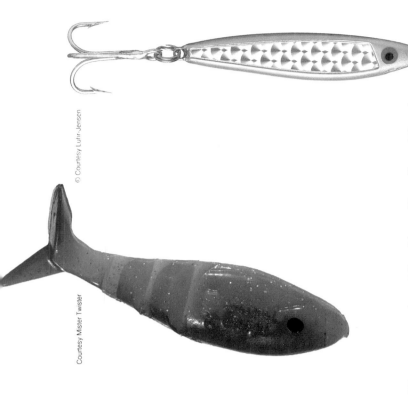

World-record fish, as defined by the International Game Fish Association (IFGA), are determined by their weight and the class line they were caught on. The IFGA keeps world records by line-strength classes—2, 4, 8, 16, 20, 30, 50, 80, and 130 pounds (1, 2, 4, 6, 8, 10, 15, 24, 35, and 60 kg). For a fish to qualify as a world record, the line it was caught on must break at or below its stated breaking point, or the fish gets pushed up into the next higher class, where it may no longer qualify as a record.

Fishermen use all sorts of tricks to entice a fish to the hook: Invisible line like this heavy-duty 23-pound (10.4-kg) test monofila-ment, BOTTOM, lures, ABOVE, and live bait, BELOW, RIGHT.

Much is made of the issue of visibility of lines. The contention is that lines that are easy for the angler to see are also easy for the fish to see, which scares them away. Clear lines, which are less likely to spook the fish, are difficult for the angler to see, making it harder for the angler to control the line. Many fish are startled to flight by shadows, particularly trout and bonefish, and many of the fluorescent lines cast shadows. A good case can be made for compromise— using clear leaders attached to colored lines—but I've always fished transparent lines myself. Fish only have two things to do most of the time: eat or be eaten. Most fish don't relish the idea of being eaten, so they take off like streaks from places where shadows suggest the possibility of predators.

One more word on the subject of line: buy the best line you can afford. It is your only connection with the fish. In my humble opinion, people who lose big fish to old or cheap lines are honor-bound to contemplate hari-kari, whether they are Japanese or not.

© Bill Staley/FPG International

Every deep-sea fisherman's dream is to come in with a catch like this.

A Word to the Wise

INSECT repellants are often crucial to an enjoyable fishing trip, given the existence of such pestiferous nuisances as mosquitoes, black flies, and such. Again, be aware that the most effective of the insect repellants, DEET (Diethyl-Toluamide), will melt fishing line or sunglasses frames or any other synthetic substance as effectively as it deters bugs. After applying DEET to all exposed portions of your body, wipe your hands carefully before handling your line. It can weaken line to the breaking point.

Perhaps this is the place to offer one more warning about DEET. The first time I fished Great Slave Lake in the Northwest Territories, I wisely applied DEET to my face and the backs of my hands. Less wisely, I drank several cups of tea at breakfast. The sun was warm as we fished, and as the morning passed, I wiped my face once or twice with my sleeve. There were no mosquitoes out in the middle of the lake, so all was well. Unfortunately, 16-foot (5-m) runabouts come equipped with a Chipewayan guide and a very nice young man as a fishing partner, but no facilities for relieving oneself. By the time we landed on one of the many lovely little islands for lunch, I was quite desperate.

The moment we landed, I leaped ashore to find an appropriately discreet bush. This was a major challenge since Arctic plants are quite stunted. I noticed, in passing, that with each step I took in the thick muskeg, clouds of mosquitoes rose around my feet. Finally sufficiently out of sight, I hurriedly unzipped my jeans. It suddenly occurred to me that there were places I had not thought to put DEET that morning. In addition, my face, having been wiped off with my sleeve, was virtually unprotected.

I am wildly allergic to insect bites. A mosquito bite the size of a pinprick on a normal person will raise a huge angry red welt on me. By the time I got back to the boat my face looked as though I'd been mugged. Later that evening, I counted 140 bites on the front of my legs and I couldn't see the backs. To say I was extremely uncomfortable truly would be an understatement. And so I say unto you, don't forget to put DEET on all the places that might be exposed. Or don't drink a lot of tea. (A word of warning: Gentlemen may wish to use caution rather than DEET on certain portions of their anatomy.)

© Robert & Linda Mitchell

OPPOSITE PAGE: Fishing on Great Slave Lake.

THIS PAGE, TOP: A Luhr-Jensen Fire Plug. MIDDLE: A Chartreuse/Flake Lure. BOTTOM: A Hot Shot.

Courtesy Luhr-Jensen

Courtesy Mister Twister

Courtesy Luhr-Jensen

The Alluring Lure; or, a Treatise on Terminal Tackle

These dandy little spinners will bring home all the fish a reasonable person could wish for or fish for. Fish are attracted by the flash and vibrations of the spinner. Spinners are supposed to look like minnows, and swivels only improve the action.

THIS may be the most important sentence in this book: *Fish don't buy lures.* Lures are designed to sell to fishermen. The companies that manufacture lures figured this out a long time ago. Ergo, lures are designed to entice fishermen, not fish. If a lure catches fish, that is a plus, as marketing people see these things. If it never catches a fish, but sells well, the marketing mavens consider themselves to have done their jobs well and will probably come out with more lures of similar design next year.

This is not to suggest that lures don't work; many do. That's part of the reason fishermen keep buying them. But it is reasonably well known in the terminal-tackle industry that half-a-dozen classic lures

will catch all the fish any reasonable person would ever hope to.

Gary Soucie, author of *Hook, Line, and Sinker*, declares, "The red-and-white Daredevle spoon has probably caught more fish in more waters for more anglers than any other single lure of a given color pattern." I wouldn't argue. The most effective minnow-imitations, or crankbaits, are the Rapala lures. Designed to imitate the action of a slightly crippled baitfish, they work so well that I regret every single one I've ever lost, even those ruined by big fish. I've caught lots of big lake trout and northern pike on Five of Diamonds spoons, and have them in several sizes. Mepps or Panther Martin spinners, typically small brass-and-feather combinations, work ex-

Red-and-white Daredevle spoons are absolutely indispensible equipment for the angler. If you have no other lure, buy this one.

Courtesy Eppinger

Courtesy Luhr-Jensen

3.

2.

1.

Courtesy Luhr-Jensen

tremely well with trout and grayling. If you fish for bass, buy a couple of poppers or plugs with big eyes painted on. Throw in some soft plastic imitations of worms or grasshoppers to complete the collection. Get these lures in several sizes, and at least two or three in the sizes you expect to use most. The toll taken by logs, rocks, trees, and the big ones that get away can be daunting, and the loss of your lures can easily end a day's fishing earlier than planned.

There are thousands of lures on the market. Some light up, some smell (the fragrances include dewberry and marmalade), some make noise, some are shiny, some are dull, some have fancy feathers, some have plastic hula skirts in fluorescent colors, some purport to emit electrical vibrations that attract fish—and I haven't even begun to touch on all the possibilities. You don't need them to catch fish.

The classic lures recommended earlier will catch everything except big saltwater gamefish like king salmon, bluefin tuna, or marlin. For these, the lodge, sportfishing boat, or guide provides the appropriate terminal tackle, so unless you go sportfishing six or seven times a year or have your own cabin cruiser, don't bother to buy it.

A little footnote on lost lures. Guide Jack Austad once took me fishing on the Tahkini River outside of Whitehorse in the Yukon Territory. We were fishing for lake trout in a pool just below a log jam. Jack mentioned that he often came there in the summer after the spring runoff and dived for lures lost by other anglers on the logs. Intrigued, I scrambled onto the jam, maintaining a precarious balance, and within a few minutes salvaged a fine collection of perfectly good lures. We cleaned them up and added them to Jack's tackle box. Then we caught our dinner and went back to his house to see if we could catch a glimpse of the moose that liked to swim across the river and graze on the grass outside his living room window.

Courtesy Cabela's

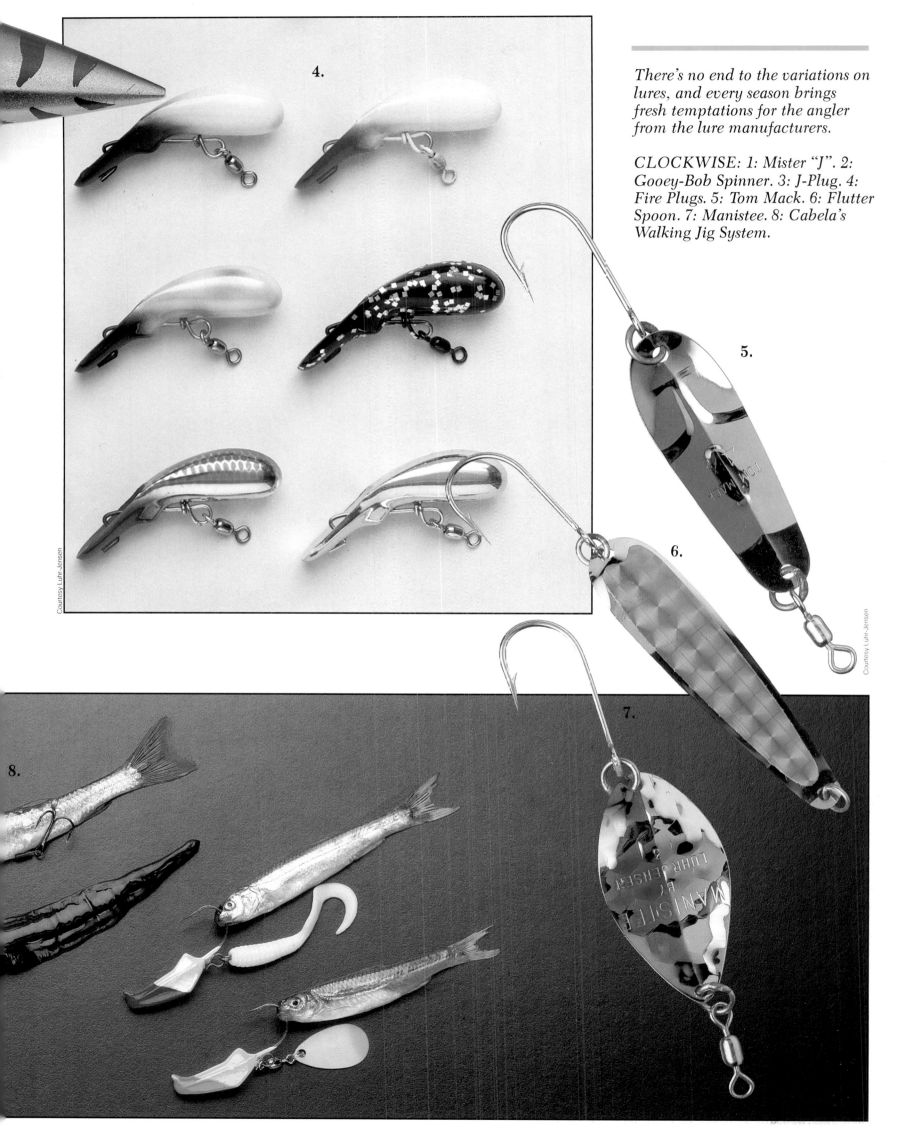

4.

5.

6.

7.

8.

There's no end to the variations on lures, and every season brings fresh temptations for the angler from the lure manufacturers.

CLOCKWISE: 1: Mister "J". 2: Gooey-Bob Spinner. 3: J-Plug. 4: Fire Plugs. 5: Tom Mack. 6: Flutter Spoon. 7: Manistee. 8: Cabela's Walking Jig System.

© Francis & Donna Caldwell

FISHERMEN love to debate the question of what makes a fish take a bait. Offered up for consideration are action, color, speed, running depth, shape, size, brightness, and pattern. Undoubtedly, all of these factors contribute something. What, precisely, it is they contribute and how important each individual element is, no one can honestly say. Obviously, if you're not fishing at the depth at which the fish are feeding, you won't catch many. Still, many a lure has caught many a fish that wasn't feeding. Neither salmon nor bass feed when they're spawning, but they'll still strike if they feel sufficiently threatened or belligerent.

Dr. James A. Henshall, whose classic *Book of the Black Bass* (1881), established the bass as America's premier sport fish, devoted an entire chapter to "Conditions Which Govern the Biting of Fish." Most of it is as sound and sensible as anything ever written on the subject, no less accurate today than the day it was written.

What Makes a Fish Take

OPPOSITE PAGE: Watching the fish explode out of water securely hooked is a large part of the fun of the sport.

ABOVE: Here's some fine bass fishing in Hell's Canyon, Idaho.

© Kenneth Martin/Amstock

Walleye like this one are superb eating.

"To seek to know all the conditions, positive and hypothetical, qualifying and exceptional, which govern the 'biting' of fish, is about as vain and discouraging a pursuit as the search for the philosopher's stone.

"To know, positively, before leaving one's office, countinghouse, or workshop for a day's outing, that it is the day of all others in the season [when] the phase of the moon, the conditions of sky and atmosphere, the direction and force of the wind, and the temperature and condition of the water are just right to insure success, and to know just what bait or fly to use, and in what portion of the stream to fish, implies a state of knowledge that can never be attained by ordinary mortals. It involves a pursuit of knowledge under such extreme difficulties, that even prescience and omniscience are but ciphers in the total sum, for it leaves out the most important factor in the calculation—the fish itself.

"Such anglers imagine that fish, somehow, form an exception to the rest of the animal creation, and are governed in their feeding or 'biting' by unchanging laws, and that these immutable laws have an outward expression in certain states and conditions of weather and water; and that it is only necessary to ascertain the peculiar combination of wind, weather and water, under which fish feed, *nolens volens* [willy nilly], to be able to effect their capture easily.

"The glorious uncertainty attending the 'biting' of fish, even at apparently favorable times, has been observed for ages, and has invested the gentle art [of fishing] with a glamour, and an air of mystery, in which the element of change, or luck, is a prominent feature. The angler wending his way homeward is accosted at every turn with the question of, 'What luck?'

"Even with all the information that can be obtained, by close and careful observation of the habits of fishes, there is still much left to be explained. And perhaps it is best so, for there has ever been a delightful uncertainty attending the angler's art, and therein lies one of its chiefest charms; for while it stimulates the angler to renewed effort, it consoles him in defeat. The pleasures of anticipation have ever exceeded those of fruition, and ever will while 'hope springs eternal in the human breast.'

"But why do fish eagerly take the bait one day, and utterly refuse it the next, when, apparently, all other conditions are equal? This is a poser, and has baffled observant anglers for ages, and will in all probability, never be solved satisfactorily."

Mister Twister, the ecologically sound plastic version of a nightcrawler, works well, even in some of the Day-Glo colors it comes in.

Cooking the Catch

SMALL fish are usually cleaned and cooked whole. Larger fish should be cleaned, scaled or skinned, and filleted. Cut just behind the gills to remove the head and just in front of the fin to remove the tail. To fillet, slit the belly from end to end, open it like a butterfly, and slice carefully along one side of the spine. Slide the knife under the spine to cut it loose, and the backbone and side bones should lift easily out. For big fish like salmon, clean the fish, remove the head and tail, and cut the body into slices three-quarters of an inch to an inch (19 to 25 mm) thick.

Salmon and trout, of course, are always the fish of choice, but bass make fine eating, too, and a mess of fresh panfish—bluegills, crappies, sunfish, or perch—are nothing to be sneered at. Figure one salmon steak, a couple of ten-inch (25-cm) trout, one half-pound (0.2-kg) bass, or half-a-dozen panfish per person. The simplest method is simply to grill the fish over a campfire. Rub the fish lightly with a little butter, or even better, bacon grease, to keep it from sticking to the grill. All it takes is a few minutes on each side to reach that peak of perfection precisely between half-raw and too dry. Fish flakes easily when it's done, so test it with a fork at the thickest part of the fish, and use a Buck knife or spatula to take it off the grill without losing half of it into the fire.

On the beach in the Yucatan, Mexican anglers peel and sharpen a slim, green stick, soak it in water, thread a fish on it, sprinkle the fish with red pepper, and roast it like a hot dog. They use strips of palm leaf to tie the fish so it doesn't slip off as it cooks, but wet string would probably work as well. To go gourmet for breakfast, wrap the fish in bacon strips pegged on with a toothpick or small stick. The fragrance of bacon, fish, and hot coffee will bring every angler for miles (km) around into camp in time to wish you a good morning, and maybe stick around for a bite to eat, if you insist. This

CLOCKWISE: Crappie, yellow perch, bluegill, and pumpkin seed all fall into the panfish category. They're fun to fish for and easy to catch.

Walleye may be had all year around if you're willing to go ice fishing for them in the winter.

© Wally Eberhart

is not a recipe for those who genuinely love solitude in the wilderness.

One of the best fish lunches I ever ate was cooked by a guide named Bart who now manages Wollaston Lake Lodge in northern Saskatchewan, Canada. It may be that I remember that lunch so fondly because for about three hours while we beat our way back to the lodge through a pounding storm, I thought it was my last meal. We did make it back to the safety of the lodge about five minutes before they sent out the search planes, and though it turned out not to be my last meal, I can attest that it was good enough to be one. Bart dotted a big lake trout with butter, stuffed it with minced onion, sprinkled it with salt and pepper, and wrapped it in three layers of aluminum foil. Just before sealing the foil, he sloshed a

© David Csepp/Ellis Wildlife Collection

Sockeye and silver salmon fillets are about as good as fish eating gets. Grilled, broiled, barbecued, poached, however they're done, no sauce beyond a squeeze of fresh lemon is required.

generous slug of excellent whiskey over the fish, and laid it in the coals to bake. That lunch was only slightly short of heaven. Baking takes longer than grilling, so figure ten minutes or more on each side. The larger the fish, the longer it takes to cook. I've varied this recipe by stuffing rainbow trout with a couple of cloves of chopped (not crushed) garlic, and sloshing it with a dry white wine or sherry.

If you have a stove and a frying pan, sauté your fish. Have the butter sizzling before you put the fish in, and turn it as soon as the skin is crisp and brown. There are lots of variations for sautéeing. Toss in some sliced onions or crushed garlic or a dash of white wine just before you add the fish. Or sauté diced ham and potatoes first, add a little more butter, then cook your fish in the same pan. The fish gets a faint hint of ham flavor that's especially good with bass. For a great breakfast fish fry, make some bacon, pour off most of the drippings, and sauté your fish in what's left.

Sometimes—O glorious moment!—you catch more fish than you can eat at once. In that case, make the lazy angler's ceviche. Skin the fish, remove the bones, and chop it into bite-size pieces. For a pound of fish (0.45 kg), you'll need ½ of a small onion (chopped), 3 tablespoons (45 ml) of olive oil, 1 cup (.24 l) of lemon juice or ¾ cup (.18 l) of lime juice, and a few leaves of coarsely chopped Chinese

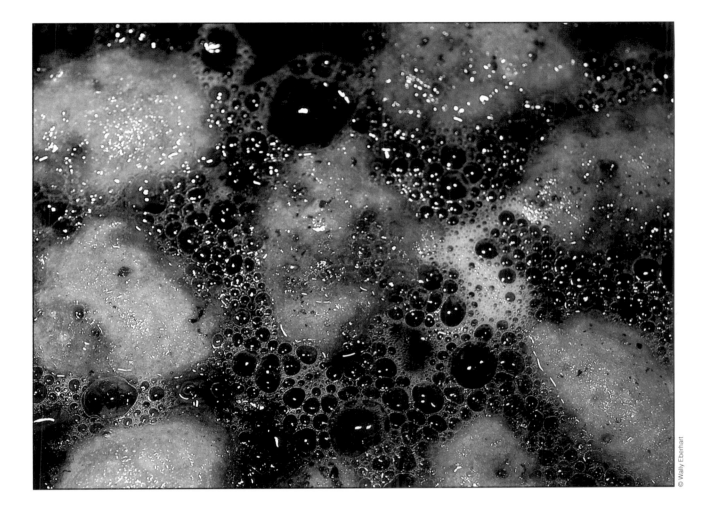

© Wally Eberhart

© Betty Groskin

parsley (cilantro). Dump it all into a zip-lock plastic bag, seal the bag tightly, and stash it in a cool place where raccoons and bears can't get it. The acid from the lemon or lime "cooks" the fish in four or five hours. All you have to do is open the bag and feast.

Obviously, some of these recipes use the sort of food you're likely to bring on a fishing trip anyway, stuff like bacon, onions, potatoes, and salt and pepper. Others, like the ceviche, take a little advance planning, since most people don't include a few sprigs of fresh cilantro on the Standard Operating Procedures provisions list, but since those few sprigs don't take up a lot of room, and you *might* catch more than you can eat at one sitting, it wouldn't hurt to have it along, just in case the action gets hot. Lemon and lime are *de rigueur* with fish no matter how they're cooked, most certainly when it's grilled or sautéed, so they're worth having along in quantities that make the ceviche possible, too.

As long as we're talking about bringing along some things that are a little out of the ordinary, add a small bottle of vinegar, 6 peppercorns, and ½ of a bay leaf to the list, and we'll go in for some serious *haute cuisine*, the sort of meal M.F.K. Fisher immortalizes from whitewashed Provençal village inns in the south of France. It's called *truite au bleu* (blue trout). Like all the best things, it's absolutely simple. Bring a quart (.95 l) of court bouillon—three parts water to one part vinegar—to a boil. Add 6 peppercorns, 1 teaspoon (5 ml) salt, ½ bay leaf, and pepper to taste. Take the trout you caught and cleaned only moments before (handle the fish gently—what turns the trick here is the slick natural coating on the fish, so you don't want to rub it off with too much handling), and plunge it into the court bouillon for four minutes. It will turn a magnificent, brilliant blue, and is superb with no more elaborate sauce than hot, melted butter. *Bon appétit!*

OPPOSITE PAGE, TOP: Deep-fried fish fillets.

OPPOSITE PAGE, BOTTOM: Here's a healthy way to eat fish—grilled outdoors. This is what eating, fishing, and living well are all about.

CHAPTER SIX

Fish Tales

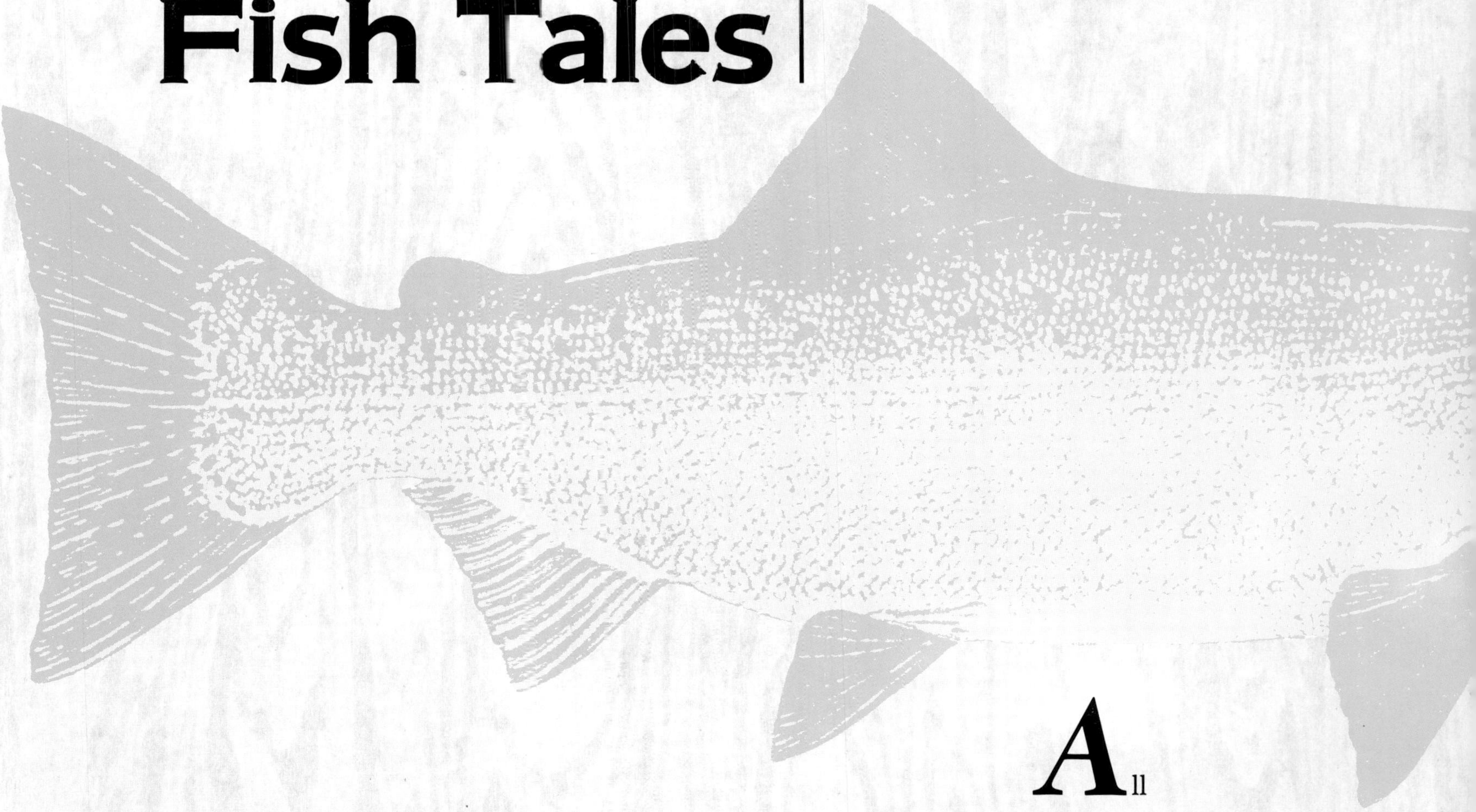

All

anglers tell tales:

some are true,

some are

taller

than true.

The tales here

are all true,

though there may

be occasions

when they stand

on tiptoe

and stretch

a little.

They are about all kinds of fish, from salmon to sturgeon, in all kinds of places, from local legends of San Francisco Bay to the Okavango Delta in sub-Sahara Africa. They are about fishing for all kinds of reasons, from feeding African fish eagles to showing off for a fifteen-year-old nephew. They are about some of the reasons that fishermen fish, but only some. It would not be possible to list all the reasons anglers angle, if only because it would sound so contradictory. Anglers fish for the pleasures of camaraderie and the joys of solitude; for fish to eat and fish to catch-and-release; to master new challenges for themselves and to show off for others; and the list goes on and on.

There are three parts to a fishing trip: the planning, the trip, and the memories. These are some of the memories.

OPPOSITE PAGE: Bluegill sunfish are known by different names in different places: sunfish, blue sunfish, bream, blue bream, copper-nosed bream, porgy sunfish, oreilles bleus, and blue joe.

ABOVE, LEFT: This pretty brook trout was taken on a Yellow Sally fly.

ABOVE RIGHT: Flounder, like halibut, are flat fish that lay on the bottom of the ocean and have a sand-colored eye side, and a white blind side. When they spawn in spring, they're often found in creeks near piers and bridges.

Of Catfish and Crocodiles

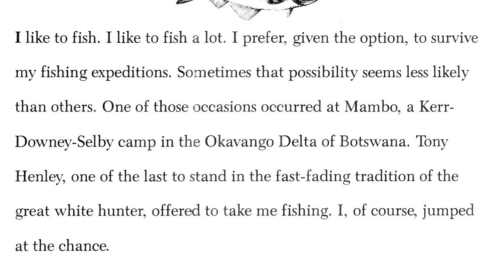

I like to fish. I like to fish a lot. I prefer, given the option, to survive my fishing expeditions. Sometimes that possibility seems less likely than others. One of those occasions occurred at Mambo, a Kerr-Downey-Selby camp in the Okavango Delta of Botswana. Tony Henley, one of the last to stand in the fast-fading tradition of the great white hunter, offered to take me fishing. I, of course, jumped at the chance.

Bundling rods, reels, lines, lures, and a handsome picnic into the Land Rover, we climbed in behind the driver and bumped off to find the river. Tony announced that we'd fish a while from the bank, have a pleasant little picnic, and then fish away the afternoon. It sounded nothing short of idyllic.

He only forgot to mention one thing. Unfortunately, it was the kind of thing that can significantly color one's perception of the day: crocodiles.

I love wading barefoot along the edge of the river. Crocodiles like it, too. I love relaxing in the sun, just absorbing the warmth. Crocodiles do too. I love swimming slowly in the river, half-submerged, half-drowsy with the heat. So do crocodiles.

We rigged our rods, and sloshed through low reeds and shallow water to the river. A small sandbar split the river in two, leaving a narrow, slow-moving stream running along before us. We could fish the middle distance for tigerfish, an African cousin of the piranha, or fish the bottom for catfish to throw to the African fish eagles, Tony said. I voted to start with the catfish, and then move into high gear with the tigerfish later. Tony cast and almost immediately hooked a nice four-pound (1.8-kg) catfish. I dropped my rod, and ran for my camera to record the fight.

Snapping away, I suddenly noticed a distinct V of water following the fight as closely as I was. "Uh, Tony," I said, trying to keep

OPPOSITE PAGE, TOP: The catfish of Africa can survive long periods out of water when their seasonal streams and ponds dry up.

my voice casual, "Uh, Tony, there's a crocodile trailing your fish."
"Yeah, they do that," he replied. I looked at Tony's legs, bare to the
cuffs of his Bermuda-length safari suit.

As the catfish flopped out of the water, the crocodile stopped at
the edge, yellow eyes taking in the menu. Tony yelled to me to bring
the hook remover, and I scampered for the Land Rover, hoping the
croc would go away in the meantime. I pulled the hook while Tony
held the fish. "That was a pretty good-sized croc," I observed.
"There's a bigger one right behind you," Tony replied. No soldier
ever did a faster about-face. Sure enough, not ten feet (3 m) away, a
much larger crocodile lay in perfect repose, basking in the sun, eyes
closed, lips curved into a small smile, looking for all the world like
one of those men on the French Riviera one's mother would not
approve of.

I had thought I was being fairly observant. I'd identified several
species of ducks, a couple of herons, a few little songbirds. I thought

*BELOW: Crocodiles are thoughtful, intel-
ligent predators. They will patiently lie in
wait day after day near a bathing place or
drinking spot before striking. They move
shockingly fast, and kill their prey by
holding it under water until it drowns.*

OPPOSITE PAGE: Striped bass.

I was paying attention. But suddenly crocodies appeared everywhere: on the bank, in the stream, on the sandbar. Every log every lump, every irregularity of the reeds, was revealed as a crocodile.

I do not consider myself a coward. I have walked the perimeter of large pans (water holes) in the Kalihari Desert, knowing there were lions near. I had, only days before, slogged through the swamps of the Okavango, which come complete with everything from leeches to hippos. I have taken dogsleds over frozen lakes in −10°F (−23°C) weather (not counting wind chill factor), and had the ice break beneath me. All that was as nothing as it dawned on me that there were crocodiles everywhere I looked. I am not ashamed to confess that I picked up my rod, trotted back to the Land Rover, and announced that I intended to stay there until Tony finished fishing.

The moral of this story is: Don't ever get so focused on the fishing that you forget about the rest of the wildlife.

Kent Diehl is a champion rodeo rider and trick roper; his personal collection of aboriginal artifacts makes museum curators salivate; he is one of the most knowledgeable appraisers of antiques on the West Coast; and he is married to a lovely woman, both brilliant and beautiful, who will undoubtedly be canonized someday, if for no other reason than the air of serene calm she maintains no matter what madness Kent happens to be engaged in. I secretly suspect that Kent is a character in a Hunter Thompson novel who somehow escaped into the real world. The most ordinary things he does end up having an odd, unexpected twist.

The Greatest Fishing Day Ever

It happens I ended a perfect day of fishing, ended by photographing my youngest daughter, Keila, next to a Pacific striped bass bigger than she was.

A few days before, after working out some new trick roping antics, my roping buddy jokingly suggested I try out my fancy rope tricks on some of the big stripers riding in on the high tides that barrel through the Golden Gate into San Francisco Bay. He clearly figured I was a better trick and fancy roper than sport fisherman. So I decided to take him up on it.

It was my very first crack at stripers, so I loaded up the car with every piece of fishing gear I owned, plus everything I could beg, borrow, or steal. I looked like every other angler that ever headed out the Gate after striper. Ropes, rods, hooks, I would take whatever was necessary, and risk all, to go after those big stripers.

My first surprise came when he told me I didn't have to be at the dock until about eight in the morning. I'd always heard that the sport-fishing boats departed promptly at five, so this announcement elicited my usual contemplative and thoughtful response: "HUH?!?" Seems he had recently become a partner in a local dealership for the twin-keeled Boston Whaler. This paragon of vessels, he assured me, could whip right out the Golden Gate so fast we'd beat the other fishing boats out to the first fishing grounds of the day. A couple extra hours of sleep is not the sort of thing a sensible person takes lightly. I followed orders.

We were the last to leave that morning: The Sausalito harbor was nothing but dead piers, still water, and empty berths. I still thought he was kidding about how fast his boat could go as we eased into San Francisco Bay. Suddenly, I was grabbing for the cockpit trim—we were flying. We must have left even the roar of the engine behind, because I don't remember any noise. Never had I gone so fast on the Bay. Out the Gate full throttle, and damned if he didn't head right for a riptide more dangerous than most. I'd have tacked to give that rip a wide berth, but my pardner smashed right in.

The magnitude riptide phenomenon only occurs in a very few places in the world. San Francisco Bay is one of them. On incoming tides, all the water in the Pacific Ocean tries to squeeze itself through the narrow opening of the Golden Gate into the Bay, and on outgoing tides, all the water in the Bay tries to run out into the ocean. The waves of the rip looked like upside-down ice cream cones, eight or nine feet (2.4 or 2.7 m) tall. Huge wind-blown tufts of white foam drenched us as the waves smashed the boat. I tightened my grip, and resigned myself to a watery grave.

My old pard thought it was child's play. Once outside the Gate that dude even spun around to enter those monsters from the ocean side, just for fun. My bronc-riding experience came in handy; I just snugged down to ride it out.

Out of the Gate full throttle, we threw a fine rooster tail through the "potato patch," the place where the Pacific Ocean and the San Francisco Bay fight each other every time the tide turns.

© Jeff Foott/Tom Stack & Associates

Elephant seals make fascinating viewing as they lie on northern California beaches.

(When we got back to the dock that evening, we were roundly berated by an older and wiser fisherman. "You crazy or something? Saw you buried in the big rip. Called the Coast Guard to come pick up the pieces, but you lucked out, I guess." "Wanna buy a real boat?" my pardner countered.)

After riding the rip, we tooled out to Duxburg Reef, full bore. We trolled here, there, and around until we caught our limit of salmon. Nice weights, no trophies, just beauties. That pretty well took care of the morning. We refueled on coffee, and watched the sun part the haze for an enchanting view of the Marin Headlands: golden hills, sea lion coves, and two beaches, Tennessee and Cronkite, glittering with carnelian and jade.

Eased up to half-throttle, we pulled out a giant sunfish. We ate
lunch off Marin's Elephant Seal beach, watching the two-ton (1.8-t)
monsters through our field glasses. Fascinating.

We slid back into the Bay and anchored in the shallows off the
north cliffs. In those days, how many rockfish you caught was determined largely by how fast you could re-bait your hook. Our legal
limit, as I recall, was well over a hundred pounds (45 kg). We hauled
in Cabezon, Boccacio, Ling Cod, and blue, yellow, and red rockfish.

About then, mid-afternoon, the tide started heading in. Throttle
forward, we set off for Mile Rock, located exactly one mile (1.6 km)
out from the Golden Gate Bridge where the old Mile Rock lighthouse stood rusting. I grabbed the rope cable ladder hanging from
the old lighthouse boom, a derelict reminder of the days when the
lighthouse had been fully manned. Years before, as a newspaper
reporter, I had interviewed the Coast Guardsmen stationed there.
They'd taken my photograph inside the huge lighthouse lens and
another of me, balancing precariously on the peak of the lighthouse
roof. Dumb, but fun. This time I climbed the swaying ladder
suspended from a rusty boom to the abandoned lighthouse in a pair
of hip boots. If I slipped, I was dead. Still dumb, but still fun. I
wandered through the vacant rooms to refresh old memories.

A big blast on the horn brought me running: the tide was roaring in. Getting down that swinging, swaying ladder was nasty
business. My pardner worked the boat under several times before
the boat, the ladder and I cinched up so I could drop aboard. The
tide was ferocious.

Ever see a freighter plow through seas at three-quarter bells?
Deep sea sailors say she has a "bone in her teeth." That's how the
old Mile Rock Lighthouse looked, but it was standing still. The
tide roared past at thirteen or fourteen knots.

TOP: *Even folks who don't fish can tell when the stripers are running by the number of boats out fishing for them in San Francisco Bay.*

BOTTOM: *Striped bass may grow up to six feet (1.8 m) long and weigh as much as 125 pounds (56.25 kg).*

We had to power hard just to stay in place. Waves split by the rock crested, and created walls of water six to ten feet (1.8 to 3 m) high and three feet (1 m) thick. In those walls flashed the forms of giant Pacific stripers. Hooks baited up with sardines, we cast in front of the huge fish. When one struck, we pulled away from the wild water around the rock to play the fish.

Tides of that magnitude don't last long, so we'd power in alongside, get a hit, pull away, lose one, boat one, bait up fast, and dash back into the fray. My pardner and I each brought in three very big striped bass. In those days, each angler could keep three stripers over sixteen inches (40 cm) long. Ours were more than twice that long, and we boated six in less than forty minutes.

Those were my first striped bass, *Roccus (Morone) saxatilis*, descendents of fry transplanted from New Jersey's Shrewsbury and Navesink Rivers to San Francisco Bay in 1879. Multiplying beyond all expectations, the striper became more abundant in the Pacific than in the Atlantic, and ranges along the West Coast from Washington to southern California. Those *Roccus (Morone) saxatilis* will always exist in my memory as huge, dark forms six feet (1.8 m) up in the waves of a raging tide, streaking after schools of sardines disoriented by finding Mile Rock where they expected more water to be.

Gill nets, overfishing, pollution, and understaffed and underpaid Fish and Game Wardens unable to keep up with increasing crowds of fishermen, have taken their sad toll. Salmon fishing is down, and now you're lucky to catch two or three rockfish in a day's fishing. Stripers are down to fewer than one million.

I don't think the tides come in as ferociously as they did twenty years ago. The lighthouse is cleaned up, automated, and serves as a helicopter pad; the old ladder fell into the deep long ago. No day of fishing has ever equalled that one. The sea is different now, I guess.

© Gregory K. Scott

A solid-frozen lake is no reason to stop fishing. Black crappie, yellow perch, burbot, and lake trout all will take a bait in winter.

Ice Fishing Quebec

THIS is probably a strange thing to confess for a person who has traveled to the Arctic three times in the last twelve months, but I hate to be cold. I'm a California kid, born and bred. California's the kind of place that even where it's cold, it isn't cold I mean, there are days we ski at Lake Tahoe in swimsuits. Serious cold, the bone-cold kind, doesn't happen a lot in California. Where I live, in Marin County, 40°F (4°C) is all it takes to make me whimper and wonder what I've done to offend the gods of warmth.

Ice fishing, as one might suspect from the name, is cold. The ice on lakes in northern Quebec freezes to four feet (1.2 m) thick and more. The fish are below the ice, often a long way below the ice, usually on the bottom of the lake. So why, you sensibly inquire, am I doing this? Because it's fishing—and it's fun.

RIGHT: With ice fishing, there's no worry about the fish spoiling. After five minutes on the ice, they are practically frozen solid.

BELOW: Hand augers take longer and are more work, but the work warms you up, which is very pleasant on days when the temperatures are well below 0°F (−18°C).

The technique is this: First you build a fish shack which is really little more than four walls and a floor around a woodstove. Then you fire up the woodstove until it's so hot in the shack that the −10°F (−23°C) temperatures outside feel refreshing.

An auger is used to drill the ice. The deluxe model is motor-driven and takes about two minutes to bore through the ice; the manual model is hand-cranked and takes significantly longer, but the work makes you warm.

Heavy-duty line is tied to the middle of a stick about three feet (1 m) long. A large lure is dropped through the hole and the line played out until it bumps the bottom. Then the line is rewound a couple of times to dangle invitingly just above the bottom when the stick is laid crosswise across the hole.

At this point, one has two choices: One can sit quietly by the hole to see if a fish takes, risking hypothermia in the process, or one can go back to the fish shack and enjoy a quiet, contemplative hour or two (read: nap, polish off a six-pack, or consider the state of the universe).

The fun part comes next. Gather up all available small children, pile them on a snowmobile behind you in a daisy-chain hug for warmth and safety, and take a run out to check the lines. One kid on either end of the stick turning it in the same direction (this is key), will soon reveal the presence of a fine, fat fish on the hook. Likely takers are lake trout (grey trout), whitefish, and burbot, a freshwater cousin of the cod.

The catch caught and cleaned, tradition requires that it be eaten immediately. One fine fish feast at which I was a grateful guest featured burbot breaded and fried, lake trout marinated in oil and onions and fried, burbot roe spiced and sautéed, sautéed onions heaped high on top of the fish, boiled potatoes, and cole slaw. The Laurentide beer and *Quebecois*-bottled wine flowed freely. The fish was good, the company was great, and it was all fine fun one cold winter day on Lac Chibougamau in northern Quebec.

BELOW, LEFT: These are truly dedicated fishermen on Lake St. Clair in Michigan in some three-pairs-of-socks weather.

BELOW, RIGHT: What's needed for ice fishing is plenty of hot coffee. At Lake Stowe, Massachusetts, they just dip the water out of the hole in the ice and boil it up.

Sturgeon Strike

DICK MURDOCK, *who tells this tale, is a well-known outdoor writer with several books to his credit, as well as a columnist for northern California newspapers. One day he went fishing for sturgeon on San Francisco Bay...*

Everything has to be just right to catch the elusive diamondback, and if you're not well prepared in every detail, chances are you'll get skunked and never know why. I'll never forget that crisp November evening back in 1983 when everything was just right. Kent Diehl and I were out on San Francisco Bay with a friendly Captain Don in his twenty-foot (6-m) runabout complete with roadster top. We were anchored just south of the Richmond-San Rafael Bridge in about twenty-eight feet (8.4 m) of water. The outgoing tide was running strong as the muddy current swirled around the stern of the runabout.

"It's getting dark," Captain Don said. "Have to be heading in pretty quick now."

"Only been out an hour," Diehl said. "Haven't got a fish yet."

"You got one pumper, Kent," I said. "If you'd been paying attention you might've nailed the critter. That bite was the classic, delicate pumping action of a big, ugly sturgeon testing your mud shrimp with his vacuum cleaner mouth."

Three limber-tipped rods rested in wooden cradles at about forty-five-degree angles, the last two or three guides of each extending beyond the wooden troughs to be uninhibited in case of a strike. Each reel held a full spool of twenty-pound (9-kg) test monofilament line. With the tide running this fast, the hefty mud shrimp lashed to 8/0 hooks with stretch thread were held to the bottom with twelve-ounce (336-g) sliding sinkers, each ninety-pound (40-kg) test short wire leader adorned with an additional rubber-core sinker to insure solid bottom contact with the bait.

OPPOSITE PAGE: White sturgeon has several other common names, all of which reflect the fact that it is found on the Pacific Coast of North America from Alaska to Monterey, California: Pacific sturgeon, Oregon sturgeon, Columbia River sturgeon, and Sacramento sturgeon. They swim upstream into Pacific Coast rivers to spawn in the spring. At maturity white sturgeon are over 12 feet (3.6 m) long and weigh as much as 1,000 pounds (450 kg). Sturgeon are slow growing, and some species live a hundred years.

Each free rod tip bent slightly to the pull of the tide. None of us had cast far. It wasn't necessary. Captain Don had tossed his bait slightly starboard, Kent straight back, while I'd angled mine a bit to the port side. Less chance of lines tangling this way. All reels had their drags set reasonably tight. We were all poised and ready, but time was running out.

"It's getting nippy," Kent said.

"And darker," Captain Don added.

"We haven't tried any of the grass or ghost shrimp we brought along for bait," I said.

"Out here mud shrimp is best," the captain said flatly. "And the most expensive."

The silhouette of Mt. Tamalpais rising out of the center of Marin County etched the fading skyline to the west with impressive magnificence. We waited silently. The only sounds were the current and the distant rumble of traffic on the bridge behind us. Our eyes were glued to our respective rod tips as we concentrated on the hope of witnessing the aforementioned delicate pumping action of a sturgeon bite.

"One more minute and we pull anchor," Captain Don said, breaking our silence.

Just as the skipper reached for his rod to reel in, Kent's rod tip dipped, raised, dipped again, gently but distinctly, Diehl dropped to his knees, raised the butt of the rod from the cradle, stood up suddenly, and rared back hard, setting the hook one, two, then three times.

Off the stern, perhaps twenty yards (18 m), the water's surface exploded. A long, white-bellied apparition pierced the fast-fading light and hung suspended a second or two before gravity drew the writhing body back into the bay with a great splash.

OPPOSITE PAGE: In fighting big fish, the captain's skills are as important as the angler's—forcing the fish to fight the weight of the boat and the hook, and keeping the line taut and the boat free of the line when turning.

"Big one," Captain Don yelled. "I'll buoy the anchor."

"Make it fast," Kent sang out. "He's stripping line, and I can't turn him."

I glanced at my watch: 6:10 P.M.

Don attached a big red plastic float to the end of the anchor line as a marker. Now the boat was free to be towed around the bay in the dark by a very large and seriously annoyed sturgeon. The big diamondback swam south with the outgoing tide. Kent battled to regain some line; there was little left on the spool. Captain Don and I helped out by shouting encouragement. I suddenly realized the lights on the west shore were the homes at Paradise Cay. That fish had hauled three people and a twenty-foot (6-m) boat two miles (3.2 km) already, and it wasn't even tired.

"Here, Dick," Kent said. "Spell me a while. I'm pooped."

As he handed me the rod, the fish changed direction and headed straight for us. I reeled madly trying to catch up, realizing full well that the fastest way to lose a fish is to give it slack line. Well, right now this guy had plenty. I prayed he was securely hooked. I prayed to feel some fight, not reel in an empty line. Time seemed to stop. Suddenly the monofilament came taut. For the first time I felt the power of the fish. No wonder Kent was pooped. At this rate I'd be the same in short order.

One thing about it: when the fish was running, it had both my strength and the weight of the boat to battle. Where were we? The western shoreline seemed closer, but I couldn't recognize any land-marks. I was sweating now and breathing hard.

"Here, Don," I said at last. "It's your turn."

And so it went. We passed the rod from hand to hand every ten or fifteen minutes. I'm not sure exactly when we realized the fish was tiring, that the battle had turned in our favor.

OPPOSITE PAGE: A glorious sunset— the perfect way to end a day of fishing.

Kent had the rod when the fish was finally cranked up alongside the boat. Captain Don and I saw its magnificent length. It would take some doing to wrestle him aboard once we had a lasso through his mouth and gills. The fish was of a different mind; he didn't think he was ready to be piped aboard. He began turning over and over, winding up line.

"There's the reason for the strong leader," Don said.

At last Don was able to thread the rope through the gills and out the mouth. With one massive heave we hoisted the fish aboard. At 7:50 P.M., the battle of a hundred minutes was over.

As the great sturgeon thrashed about, I noticed we were close to the National Marine Fisheries station, about four miles (6.4 km) south of where we started. That fish had dragged us four miles (6.4 km) due south, and who knows how far when he'd made his run toward the boat. That's a long way to swim towing a twenty-foot (6-m) runabout with a roadster top for drag.

Captain Don kicked the boat into gear and off we went in search of the anchor. We found the big red ball bobbing quietly in the dark, and brought it aboard. Back at the dock we agreed to tie the big fish, still alive and fighting, to a ring in a vacant berth to take pictures and vital statistics the following day.

Next morning, we managed to weigh and measure the critter, a real chore as he was fully revived. That ugly old diamondback was 6'2½" (186.3 cm) long and weighed 124 pounds (56 kg).

About then a friend who had a boat docked nearby happened along. "Nice fish," he said. "What happens next?"

"Ask Diehl," I said. "He caught him."

"Guess we'll divide and eat it," Kent said.

My friend smiled, "Got a better idea," he said. "Wait here a minute."

He ran down the dock and promptly returned bearing a big platter covered with aluminum foil. Peeling back the foil, he revealed fifty or more beautiful white sturgeon steaks.

"I'm a conservationist," he said. "Turn that fish loose and I'll give you these steaks. These are off a fish, maybe seventy-five pounds (34 kg). Better eating."

All eyes turned to Kent. He looked at the big diamondback writhing at his feet, then back to the platter. Suddenly he kneeled down, pulled the lasso free, and gave the fish a mighty shove off the dock. With a lively swish of its tail, it disappeared into the depths.

Sometimes releasing a big one is the better part of sportmanship, just as discretion is sometimes the better part of valor.

A Tyee for Todd

King salmon at sea range throughout the North Pacific. When spawning, they often run upstream several hundred miles inland. They migrate more than 5,000 miles (8,000 m), and find their way back to the stream in which they were born by smell.

SOMETIMES my fishing trips don't come at the most convenient times. One that I remember as particularly inconvenient came in the middle of a family reunion. It was the first family reunion we'd ever held on the West Coast, and as it happened, it was held at my house. As it further happened, the reunion was not for my family, but my husband's, and I was especially anxious to make everyone feel welcome. But the opportunity came up to fish for trophy king salmon from a floating fishing lodge in British Columbia called North Pacific Springs, and I couldn't bring myself to turn it down.

One of the people attending the reunion was our fifteen-year-old nephew Todd. Todd and I had done a little fishing together in Colorado a few years before, but we hadn't done very well since the Frying Pan River was in full flood. I'd sent Todd postcards from my various fishing trips telling him how it was going—what I'd caught, how many, and how big—but the fact remained, he had no proof. Todd had yet actually to lay eyes on a fish I'd caught that amounted to anything worth writing home—or him—about.

I spent two days with the family, and then hopped the plane for North Pacific Springs. The Air Canada flight got me as far as Vancouver where I was to meet my fishing partner, Russ Johnson. Russ and I had never met, but a mutual friend told me to look for Clark Kent and I couldn't miss him. As it turned out, that was a perfect description and I had no trouble picking Russ out of the crowd at the airport. It was late in the day and we were both tired when we got to the River Inn, so Russ suggested taking a bit of time to freshen up before we talked tyee—trophy king salmon—over dinner.

The room had a lovely view out over the river; it had a nice, big, bed; and on the bed was the thickest, softest, most enticing white terry cloth bathrobe that can be imagined. I thought I'd put on that bathrobe for just a moment. I thought I'd lie down on the bed for just a minute. I thought maybe I'd close my eyes for just a second. When the phone finally jarred me awake, it was Russ, and I was half an hour late to meet him for dinner. How do you explain to a virtual stranger that you were late for dinner because you were seduced by a bathrobe? But as one would expect of Clark Kent, Russ was very nice about it.

A float plane flew us over the Inland Passage to Blackfish Bay where the North Pacific Springs Lodge was anchored. Blackfish is the local name for killer whales (*Orca*), but I was not lucky enough to see any; I was too busy concentrating on catching chinook, the local name for king salmon.

Perhaps I am alone in my agonies of self-doubt, but no matter how many fish I've caught, I always worry that I'll never land another. Of course, the fish conspire to contribute to this fear. Sometimes hours pass without so much as a nibble. Sometimes, no matter how accurately I cast, no matter how exquisitely the herring is filleted, no matter how cleverly estimated the proper depth and

If it's not a tyee (king salmon over 30 pounds [13.5 kg]), *RIGHT*, it's certainly a smiley (king salmon over 20 pounds [9 kg]), *BELOW*. This was clearly a good day's fishing.

trolling speed, you'd think I was fishing in Death Valley. Nothing takes. I am haunted by two, equally terrifying, possibilities: Either there are no fish down there or they have all decided to play bridge this afternoon.

Most anglers are driven to whimpering distraction by this phenomenon, I among them. We whisper to the fish to bite as though bent on seduction; we croon to them as though trying to persuade a truculent child; in the end, we swear and sulk. All this is by way of explanation that when I caught my first fish of the day, a paltry three-pound (1.4-kg) coho, I am ashamed to admit I kept it because I was afraid I'd catch nothing else.

We trolled off the kelp beds and jagged rocks of a small heavily wooded island. An expedition of sea kayakers in brightly colored anoraks paddled between the island and the shoreline trying to choose which pretty beach to camp on for the night. Huge white cruise ships, virtual floating cities, made our sixteen-foot (4.8-m) runabouts look tiny and fragile by comparison. We set downriggers to keep the bait down, and then laboriously hauled them back up again to check the state of the bait. I scanned the shoreline for bear with my binoculars after extracting solemn promises from both Russ and the guide that they would not take their eyes off the rod tips in case we got a hit.

I needn't have worried so. When king salmon strike, there's not a lot of doubt about it. And when the hit came, Russ grabbed the rod while I reeled in the other line to keep the way clear. It took a few minutes, but he boated a handsome twenty-four pounder (11 kg). I was as pleased as he was because it proved two things: There *were* fish down there and they *weren't* all playing bridge.

Now Russ is a lifelong fisherman, skilled and knowledgeable, who had fished North Pacific Springs several times before. Every

Few things in life match the thrill of catching an Alaskan tyee.

time he'd caught fine, big salmon, but he'd never hooked into a tyee. A tyee is a king salmon over thirty pounds (13.5 kg). And that's what Russ wanted to catch this time. North Pacific Springs Lodge gives out trophy pins for kings over thirty pounds (13.5 kg), forty pounds (18 kg), and fifty pounds (22.5 kg), and probably right on up the scale, since kings can go to more than ninety pounds (40.5 kg)—the world record, caught in Alaska, is a little over ninety-two pounds (41.4 kg). Russ set his heart on one of those little round black-and-gold pins.

We re-baited the hooks and got the lines back in the water. I kept sneaking peeks at Russ's fish, heavy and handsome, gleaming bright silver in the afternoon sun. We had not trolled long when we got another strike. It was a good fight and a good fish. I landed a fine king salmon a couple pounds (.9 kg) shy of Russ's. The fading light and sinking sun sent us scurrying back to the lodge for dinner, a feast of fresh Dungeness and King crab, huge shrimp, and enormous steaks. You couldn't go hungry at North Pacific Springs if you tried, though why anyone would want to try, I can't imagine.

The next morning, I was practically twitching with anticipation. The one king I'd caught only whetted my appetite. It had fought hard and well—what would an even bigger fish fight like? I prayed for a chance to find out.

The fishing was fast that morning, at least on the other boats. We watched as most of the other boats hauled in big ones. Russ was muttering the weird incantations that fishermen traditionally mutter in hopes of compelling a fish to strike by sheer force of will. He landed a beautiful clean shining fish a little under twenty pounds (9 kg). Then, another. For some reason, all the fish were hitting on "his" side of the boat—my rod never so much as twitched. We agreed simply to trade off every other strike. Just before noon, that same rod dipped heavily. Ever the gentleman, Russ handed me the rod. "It's a big one," he said. As soon as I took the rod, I knew it was the biggest fish I'd ever played. And beyond that, I don't remember much. I have never focused so tightly on anything else in my life. All I knew was that I wanted that fish, and if I lost it, please make it because the fish was huge, and not because I played it badly.

Steelhead are sea-run rainbow trout, and grow substantially larger than their freshwater cousins. They are also known as Kamloops trout, silver trout, arc-en-ciel, and in Japan, nijimasu. Hard-fighting and great eating, steelhead are one of the world's great sport fish.

Smooth water, mist rising, luminous sky, and the chance of catching some salmon too.

I kept my rod tip up and let him run line off the reel. The instant I felt the slightest slackening of the pressure, I cranked for all I was worth. I believe Russ and the guide were shouting encouragement and instructions to me in the beginning. I know that after a few minutes it was absolutely silent. The guide manuevered the boat expertly as the fish ran first for one side and then for the other. Once Russ helped me lift the line over the motor on the back. But nobody spoke.

In my head, I pleaded with the fish to just let me see it. It ran hard away from the boat. It shook its head fiercely, determined to throw the hook. It sounded, running line off the reel at a fearsome rate. I prayed not to do anything wrong, not to make any stupid mistakes. I pumped and cranked steadily, hoping to tire the fish. Suddenly it broke and ran for the boat. I reeled frantically to bring the line taut again. I have no idea whether it was sunny or overcast, warm or cold: Every cell was concentrated on playing the biggest fish I'd ever had.

It seemed as though I'd never gain on it. My arms ached and my hands were stiff. When I finally brought it close to the boat, it gave a huge leap, spraying bright water in all directions, and certifying what we already knew: it was a magnificent tyee. The sight of the boat only renewed the king's will to fight. It sounded again, and I was helpless to stop the run or turn the fish.

I have no idea how long I actually fought that fish. Russ said it was close to forty-five minutes. When the guide finally slipped the net under it, he estimated it at about forty pounds (18 kg); in fact, it was forty-one and a half pounds (18.7 kg) according to the scale back at the lodge. Russ took a photo of me holding the fish, but the truth is, the guide is standing behind me, helping me hold it up high enough to see its full length: it looks nearly as big as I am. It was the biggest king salmon caught in the three days I was there, and I was as proud of that fish as I might have been if I'd invented fish and fishing all by myself. When I was given my little black pin with its gold leaping salmon and the words *40 Trophy King* you'd have thought I'd been awarded a MacArthur Fellowship, and maybe the Nobel Peace Prize, too.

We went on to catch more king salmon that day, but we never hooked into another tyee. The next morning we went out for a last fling before the float plane flew us back to everyday reality. I caught one more tyee, a handsome thirty-four-pounder (15.3-kg). I collected another pin, this time one that read *30 Trophy King*. Russ never did catch a tyee, though he came within a few ounces of earning a thirty-pound (13.5-kg) pin. Sometimes life isn't fair, but I have to admit I like getting more than my share.

I kept only four fish of all I caught, the little three-pound (1.4-kg) coho, the two tyee and one a little more than twenty pounds (9 kg), and I still took home more than my weight in salmon.

But then a new dilemma arose. North Pacific Springs cleans the catch and offers to cut it into steaks, fillets, or head-and-tail it. Then it's packed in ice in Sytrofoam™ boxes and shipped on home with the happy angler. Except this happy angler did not, most emphatically *did not*, want that forty-one-and-a-half-pound (18.7-kg) tyee, my own personal trophy king salmon, cut into steaks or filleted or head-and-tailed. I wanted to take it home whole to show Todd. And that fish didn't even begin to fit in one of their Styrofoam™ boxes. They eventually cobbled together a custom-made container from pieces of Styrofoam™ and duct tape to cover the parts that protruded magnificently from the largest box they had, and thus it flew to San Francisco.

I think Todd believes I can fish now. I sent him and his family home to Nebraska with about thirty pounds (13.5 kg) of salmon that they say made a great barbecue for their friends and neighbors. The trophy pins are safely stowed in a small, Russian lacquer box on the Regency tea table in my living room. On occasions when the talk turns to fishing, as it does every now and again, I open the little black box and shamelessly show off those two little pins.

A few images that linger in one's memory: the patterns of light on the water, the richness of the forest's green, the sound of the water rippling over rocks, the challenge of reading the water accurately, the everlasting mystery of the unseen fish...

The Suburban Steelhead

BY and large, humans have not been good neighbors to other species. We didn't used to care. Today our thinking has been much revised, and enormous numbers of people have come to believe that we must be stewards of the earth and not heedless masters. The changes come slowly, but the earth will heal itself if we allow it to.

There is a small creek that runs through Ross, California, called Corte Madera Creek. When the rains come heavily, the creek overflows its banks and floods the houses and streets built along its orders. In the early seventies, the Army Corps of Engineers decided to dredge out the creek and replace it with a huge concrete channel to control the flooding.

Many people in the town protested that the project would destroy the salmon and steelhead that ran up the stream to spawn. They argued that the sea lions that came up, barking, from the Bay would come no more. They asked what would happen to the deer, raccoons, possum, and the odd, shy fox that depended on the creek for water if the channel was dug 15 feet (4.5 m) down and lined with six-foot (1.8-m) chain-link fences. Their protests were for nought. The huge bay trees at the water's edge were felled, the blackberry vines that tumbled exuberantly down the banks were ripped out. The channel was dug, the concrete poured. The forest animals sought water elsewhere. The fish no longer came upstream. With no life in the stream, the algae grew uncontrollably, until the Army Corps of Engineers deemed it necessary to drain the stream to poison the algae.

But the channel didn't work, as the townspeople had told the Corps it wouldn't. In 1982 and 1984, the rains poured down, the creek overflowed and flooded the streets to a depth of five feet (1.5 m). Plans for dredging further up the creek were protested, delayed, fought on every side. A few years ago the local chapter of Trout

Steelhead trout have demonstrated that they'll come back to spawn in streams that are cleaned up and restored.

© Don C. Carey/Cyr Color Photo Agency

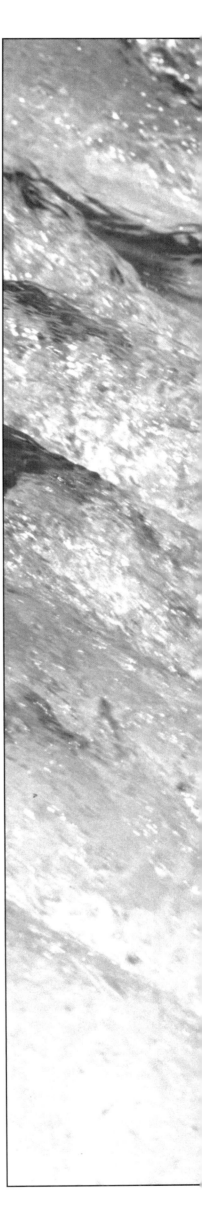

Unlimited, a national conservation organization, built fish ladders in the creek, where it winds through the high-school campus, through the meadow where the old Town and Country Club used to be, and continues to where the bridge crosses Canyon Road in the Cascades neighborhood of Fairfax. Steelhead fry were planted, and everyone waited to see what would happen.

Oldtimers told stories of a salmon run of a thousand silver salmon up that little creek, of good steelhead runs. Only ten pair of steelhead had been counted the whole length of Corte Madera Creek in 1979; by 1986 there were five hundred pair. That count is down now, what with four years of poor rains and little water released from the reservoirs—Marin County is the only county in the entire country solely dependent on rain for its water—but it's still ten times what it was in 1979.

Yesterday I stopped to watch the goldfinches eat the pollen off the pussywillows by the creek behind the post office. And then I saw it, a big steelhead, easily two feet (60 cm) long, returning to the sea after spawning upstream. It held in a sunny patch of water just above the fish ladder that links the ugly concrete channel with the creek, occasionally flashing the silver on its belly. My husband watched with me—he was the one who'd seen it first—and as we watched three bicyclists came to look, too, and then a woman who sounded triumphant when she told us that she'd been fighting the Army Corps of Engineers for twenty years. "We *told* them there were fish in the creek," she said, "but they wouldn't believe us. Now they're back. And sometimes the sea lions swim up the creek, barking."

We all held onto the chain-link fence trying to see the fish better, and grinned at each other. The steelhead had come back. Maybe someday, with enough rain to fill the creek and enough people to protect them, the silver salmon will come back, too.

To live as loving stewards, to do no further harm, to repair whatever we can of the damage we have done the earth, is the finest legacy we can leave our children, that they may know the abundance, the wildness that once was.

Glossary

A

Action: used to describe 1. the flexibility and power of a rod; 2. the swimming movement of a lure; 3. how well the fish are biting.

Anadromous: fish that are born in freshwater, swim out to sea, and return to their home stream to spawn, such as salmon and steelhead trout; sea-run fish.

Aquatic insects: insects that complete some portion of their life cycle under water.

Attractor: an unnatural fly pattern; also, any bright color in a fly that causes it to look unusual.

B

Backing: a line attached to the reel spool, used to extend the length of the fishing line. If a fish has run your line out to the backing, you're in trouble.

Bank: the high, steep sides of a stream or river.

Bar: a mound of sand, gravel, or rock that sticks out of the water or is only slightly below the surface.

Barb: the small point that protrudes just below the main point of a hook; its purpose is to embed the hook more firmly.

Barbless hook: hooks made without the barb or hooks that have had the barb clipped off. Some trout streams require the use of barbless hooks, especially for catch-and-release fishing. They are generally considered more sporting.

Bass: 1. true bass include white bass, and yellow bass, which are generally lumped with panfish; 2. members of the sunfish family, including largemouth bass and smallmouth bass, both of which are also called black bass.

Beaching: landing a fish by leading it with the line to a bar or shore where it runs aground; sometimes easier than trying to maintain your balance in a rushing stream on slippery rocks while holding a fishing rod and wielding a landing net.

Bug: a floating bass lure that imitates big insects, frogs, mice, and other natural bass prey.

C

Cast: in the United States, the act of tossing the lure to the fish with a rod and line; in Great Britain, the leader tied to the line at one end and the fly at the other.

Catch-and-release: unhooking all fish caught and returning them unharmed to the water; required on some trout streams, along with barbless hooks.

Char: a family of fish that includes the brook trout, lake trout, Dolly Varden, and arctic char.

Chumming: throwing food in the water to attract fish.

Cold-water fish: fish that thrive in water ranging from 40° to 60°F (4.4° to 15.6°C) such as salmon, trout, grayling, and char.

Cool-water fish: fish that do best in water ranging from 55° to 70°F (13° to 21°C) such as northern pike, walleye, whitefish, shad, smallmouth bass, and striped bass.

Creel: traditionally, a wicker basket with a shoulder strap for carrying a mess of trout prettily wrapped in damp ferns to keep them cool and fresh; today, it's more likely to be a fanny bag of insulated canvas or urethane-coated nylon, but the purpose is the same.

D

Dap: to lie silently on one's belly and delicately drop one's line onto the water from a ledge overhanging the stream where a very large trout might logically be expected to lie.

Density: describes the weight of a fly line (specific gravity) as compared to the weight of water. High density (*fast-sinking*) lines are heavier than water and sink quickly; low density (*slow-sinking*) lines sink slowly or not at all, in which case they're called *floating lines*.

Drag: 1. the mechanism on a reel that adjusts the amount of tension on the line; 2. the pull of the wind or current on a fly that causes it to move unnaturally; 3. friction where the line rubs against the guides on the rod.

Dress: to waterproof the fly, leader, or line to make it float.

Dun: 1. the first adult stage of mayflys (technically, subimago stage); 2. the dull gray or brown color typical of the subimago.

E

Eddy: the slowly swirling water upstream of rocks, logs, or other obstructions; fish often hold in eddies.

F

Fish on: what you get to yell when a fish takes your bait. Good manners require other anglers in the same boat to reel in their lines so you have a clear field in which to play your fish. You, of course, extend the same courtesy to others. Losing a fish because your line got tangled in someone else's does not promote amity or world peace.

Floatant: a wax or oil-based preparation used to waterproof lines, leaders, or flies to make them float.

Freshwater: 1. water with little or no salt content; 2. fish found only in freshwater.

Fry: the first stage of life for fish, usually from one-half inch to two inches (12 to 50 mm) long.

G

Gaff: a hook with a wooden handle used to land large fish; also used as a verb to describe the process of landing a fish this way.

Gap: the distance between the shank of the hook and the point.

Gills: the flaps just behind a fish's head through which it breathes.

H

Hackle: the neck and back feathers of various birds such as chicken, grouse, and partridge, used to make flys.

Handle: 1. on the rod, the part you hold to cast fish, and fight a fish; 2. on the reel, the part you crank to retrieve line.

Herl: any material used to wrap flies onto a hook.

Hold: a place where fish such as salmon, trout, or bass rest or remain stationary; the fish's territory. Reading the water consists largely of looking for likely places for fish to hold, and fishing them.

Hook eye: the closed loop on a hook to which the tippet or leader is tied.

Hookkeeper: the small eyelet at the front of a fly rod that holds the hook when you're not fishing.

Hook size: determined by the distance between the point and the shank of the hook. Hook sizing has been very confusing over the years but manufacturers are now trying to introduce some uniformity by using the Redditch scale, by which the largest hooks have the lowest numbers, the smallest hooks the highest numbers, i.e. a #1 hook is the largest, a #36, the smallest. Another whole scale exists for very large hooks on which the largest hooks have the highest numbers, i.e. 5/0, the "0" signifying "Ocean."

J

Jack: one- or two-year-old sexually mature male salmon that join the spawning run of older fish.

Jigging: twitching a line up and down to arouse a fish's curiosity and entice it to bite.

Jump: when a hooked fish leaps out of the water trying to shake the hook or break the leader.

K

Kelt: salmon running downstream to the sea after spawning.

Knotless: a leader that comes with looped ends that can be linked to the tippit and line without tying knots.

L

Land: to bring a hooked fish to the angler's hand, landing net, boat, or shore; to capture.

Lie: a fish's resting place and feeding territory; its home.

Light tackle: using light rods, low test line, and barbless hooks for fishing. This is true sportsman's angling—it gives the fish a fighting chance; it's also more fun, particularly when fishing for fish under ten pounds (4.5 kg), because the light tackle lets you really feel the fight.

Lure: anything with hooks attached that's designed to catch fish: including spoons, spinners, bugs, plugs, and poppers.

M

Mending: using the rod to lift or roll the fly line to prevent the fly from dragging.

Minnow: the generic term for any small fish from one to eight inches (2.5 to 20 cm) long.

Monofilament: a single strand of nylon used for lines, leaders, and tippets.

Mooching: fishing from a boat at anchor or drifting slowly while twitching the line every now and then to give the bait more action.

Muddler: a fat, funny-looking, and very effective fly with a clipped deer-hair head and hair and feather wings.

N

Net: to land a fish by scooping it up in a handheld landing net.

Nymph: 1. the immature stage of aquatic insects; 2. any artificial fly that imitates these insects.

P

Palming the reel: pressing the palm of your hand against the outer spool flange of a flyreel to increase the drag when a fish is running line off the reel too fast.

Panfish: refers to a number of different species of freshwater gamefish, typically under two pounds (0.9 kg), including sunfish, bluegill, crappie, yellow perch, and white bass.

Parr: another name for fingerling trout and salmon; the large dark bands or oval marks on their sides are *parr* marks.

Perch: a family of fish that includes yellow perch and walleye; it does *not* include white perch, which is a member of the bass family.

Pike: a family of cool- and cold-water gamefish with razor-sharp recurved teeth including northern pike, pickerel, and muskellunge. Walleyed pike are not pike, but perch.

Pocket: a depression on the bottom of a stream, often beneath a riffle, where fish like to hold.

Point: 1. a narrow bit of land that juts out into a stream or lake; 2. the sharp part of a hook.

Polaroids: polarized sunglasses that filter out certain angles of light to make it easier to see fish underwater.

Pound test: the weight at which line will break; sometimes simply called *test*. Fishing light tackle means to catch a fish that weighs more than the pound test, i.e. taking a four-pound (1.8-kg) fish on two-pound (0.9-kg) test line, which requires a great deal more finesse on the part of the angler since the fish could break free at any moment.

Power: 1. the energy of the arm-and-wrist movement in the forward motion of casting a fly; 2. how effectively a rod casts, hooks, and plays a fish.

Presentation: how an artificial fly lands on the water when cast; also the fly's action on the water.

Pumping: lowering the rod toward the water while reeling furiously to gain line on a large fish.

Pupa: the cocoon-like stage between the larva and adult stages of aquatic insects such as caddis and midge; the artificial fly that looks like this stage.

Put down: scaring the fish off so they no longer feed or rise to the bait; such fish have been *put down*.

R

Rapids: fast-moving water over rocks. Pools at the bottom of rapids are often good fishing.

Reading the water: looking at the water to figure out where the fish are likely to be *vis-à-vis* pools, riffles, pockets, rocks, bars, logs, or weeds.

Reel: holds the line and retrieves it.

Riffle: fast-flowing, shallow water moving over small rocks so the surface of the water ripples; wind can also riffle the water.

Rise: a fish coming to the surface to feed; leaves little concentric circles where it has risen and broken the surface. The British, having gentle, slow-moving streams, only cast to a rising fish; Americans, who must fish faster water, fish the water, that is, all the places fish are likely to be, in order to tempt them to rise.

Run: 1. what a fish does when it first realizes it's been hooked: it swims in the opposite direction as fast as it can go; 2. the stretch of stream between the end of a riffle and the pool beneath.

S

Selective: the nice term for fish that are picky eaters.

School: the correct term of venery for a group of fish of the same species swimming *en masse*; also a verb meaning to group.

Slack: what you get in your line when you don't maintain the tension between the fish and the rod. Slack line costs more anglers fish than any other single error, because the slack allows the fish to throw the hook. That's why everyone yells at you to keep your rod tip up when you have a fish on: to prevent slack.

Smolt: the name for sea-run fish such as salmon, trout, and char when they get from four to ten inches (10 to 25 cm) long; their third-stage of development.

Snagging: hooking a fish anywhere other than in the mouth. Such a fish is foulhooked, and unless too badly injured to survive, should be released immediately.

Snag guard: a device on a fly or lure intended to prevent it from snagging on things like logs, rocks, branches, trees, hats, jackets, or ears. Like weed guards, they are of dubious value.

Snelled hook: a hook or fly that comes with a short, permanent piece of monofilament tied to it so you don't have to get out your glasses to thread the tippit or leader through the microscopic hole on the hook or fly. The snell has a loop at the other end to attach to the leader.

Spawn: what fish do for sex: the hen lays the eggs and the cock swims over and sprays them with milt.

Spawning run: the movement of sea-run fish from the sea up rivers and streams to reproduce.

Spinner: 1. the second adult stage (imago) of mayflies; 2. a shiny bit of metal that attracts fish by revolving wildly when pulled through the water as part of a lure.

Spinning: casting a lure off a fixed-spool reel from which the line is pulled off by the weight of the lure; spin casting.

Splice: connecting two sections of line to each other.

Spook: scaring the fish off.

Steelhead: a rainbow trout that ran away to sea.

Still fishing: pier fishing, bank fishing, ice fishing; where the line is simply dropped in the water.

Streamer: big, brightly colored flies fished underwater, most often for salmon or saltwater fish.

Strike: 1. the fish taking the hook; 2. the act of setting the hook by jerking upward on the rod to embed the hook more firmly in the fish's mouth when the fish bites.

Stringer: a length of cord or chain for keeping caught fish alive. You thread it through one gill and out the mouth and hang it in the water. Good for carrying fish home if you have Tom Sawyer fantasies and don't have far to walk.

Stripping: pulling in a fly line with your hand when you can't reel fast enough to maintain enough tension on the line to prevent slack.

Structure: anything solid in the water that a fish might live near: weedbeds, jetty points, reefs, rocks, logs, and shoreline. Usually used in reference to lakes rather than streams.

T

Tackle: all your fishing gear from your rod and reel to your waders and float tube.

Tail: 1. the caudal fin of a fish; 2. the downstream end of a pool.

Tailing: 1. a fish feeding in water sufficiently shallow that its tail sticks above the surface; 2. landing a hooked fish by grabbing it just in front of its tail.

Take: when the fish bites it *takes* the hook.

Taking: a *taking* fly or lure is one that catches a lot of fish.

Taper: used to describe the shape of a fly-line, leader, or rod that narrows at one end.

Terminal Tackle: includes hooks, sinker, swivels, lines, leaders, tippits, lures, and knots.

Terrestrial: an insect that lives on land, such as ants, beetles, grasshoppers, and crickets.

Tide: the regular rising or lowering of water levels due to gravitational forces.

Tie: 1. the process of making artificial flies for fly fishing; 2. connecting lines, leaders, tippets, and hooks with knots.

Tippet: the small end of a leader or an exceptionally thin, clear piece of nylon monofilament tied between the leader and the hook; its purpose is to be invisible to fish so the leader and line don't spook the fish.

Treble hook: three points with barbs attached to a single shank.

Trolling: fishing by dragging a line and lure behind a boat at a speed comparable to the speed of a baitfish.

Trout: a family of freshwater gamefish found in cold, pure water, including rainbow trout, brown trout, cutthroat trout, Sunapee trout, and golden trout. Rainbow trout that are anadromous are called steelhead; cutthroat trout that do the same are called sea-run cutthroat. Sea-run fish tend to be substantially bigger than their freshwater cousins. Lake trout, Dolly Varden, and brook trout are all char, and not trout, officially.

W

Wading: walking in water no deeper than your chest to fish.

Waders: combination of waterproof shoes and overalls used for wading.

Wading staff: used to poke around at the stream bottom for holes, snags, and slippery rocks so you know why you fell when you fall.

Warm-water fish: fish that thrive in water from 65° to 85°F (18° to 30°C) such as largemouth bass, panfish, and catfish.

Wind knot: a simple overhand knot that gets accidentally tied in the leader in the process of casting. Clip the leader from the fly line and cut the knot from the leader or replace the leader.

Woolly Worm: 1. caterpillar; 2. fuzzy sinking flies that imitate caterpillars.

Bibliography

Anderson, Sheridan. *The Curtis Creek Manifesto: Being a Basic Guide to the Art of Fly Fishing on Moving Water.* Portland, Oregon: Frank Amato Publications, 1982.

Berners, Dame Juliana. *A Treatise Upon Fishing With a Hook.* New York: North River Press, 1979. (First published as *Book of St. Albans*, 1496.)

Cooper, Gwen and Haas, Evelyn. *Wade a Little Deeper, Dear: A Woman's Guide to Fly Fishing.* California Living, 1979.

Day, Bunny. *Catch 'Em, Hook 'Em & Cook 'Em.* New York: Gramercy Publishing Company, 1980.

Flick, Art. *Master Fly-Tying Guide.* New York: Crown, 1972.

Haig-Brown, Roderick. *A Primer of Fly Fishing.* New York: Morrow, 1964.

Haig-Brown, Roderick. *A River Never Sleeps.* New York: Winchester Press, 1974.

Heilner, van Campen. *Wondrous World of Fishes.* Washington, D.C.: National Geographic Society, 1965.

Henshall, Dr. John Alexander. *Book of the Black Bass.* Cincinnati: Robert Clarke & Co., 1881. (Reproduced by Bass Anglers Sportsman Society of America, 1987.)

Johnson, Osa. *Four Years in Paradise.* New York: Garden City Publishing Co., 1941.

Koller, Larry. *The Treasury of Angling.* New York: Ridge Press, 1963.

Lyons, Nick (Ed.). *Fishermans's Bounty.* New York: Crown Publishers, 1970.

MacLean, Norman. *A River Runs Through It.* Chicago and London: The University of Chicago Press, 1976.

Marbury, Mary Orvis. *Favorite Flies and Their Histories.* Hong Kong: The Wellfleet Press, 1988. (First published 1892.)

McClane, A.J. *Field and Stream International Fishing Guide.* New York: Holt, Rinehart, & Winston, 1971. (This is updated and reprinted every couple of years.)

Schwiebert, Ernest W. *Matching the Hatch.* New York: Macmillan, 1955.

Schwiebert, Ernest W. *Trout.* New York: E.P. Dutton, 1978.

Soucie, Gary. *Hook, Line and Sinker: The Complete Angler's Guide to Terminal Tackle.* New York and London: Simon and Schuster, 1982.

Traver, Robert. *Trout Madness.* New York: St. Martin's Press, 1960.

Tryckare, Tre and Cagner, E. *The Lore of Sportfishing.* New York: Crown Publishers, 1976.

Walton, Izaak and Cotton, Charles. *The Compleat Angler.* London: The Folio Society, 1959 (First published 1653.)

Whitlock, Dave. *L.L. Bean Fly-Fishing Handbook.* New York: Nick Lyons Books, 1983.

Wulff, Lee. *The Atlantic Salmon.* New York: Nick Lyons, Books, 1983.

PRESERVING and protecting the water and wildlife is the only way we can hope to fish in the future. Streams, rivers, lakes, and bays throughout North America have been ruined as suitable habitat for fish by siltation caused by deforestation and overgrazing; by poisoning from effluent pollution and acid rain; by thermal pollution which changes water temperatures until the fish can no longer survive; by water levels drastically altered by water diversion projects such as dams and aqueducts; and by overfishing. Many steps have been taken to heal the damage done and more are being taken every day.

We cannot dam and divert every wild river on the continent and expect to have any fishing to speak of. We can no longer afford the luxury of behaving as arrogant and reckless tenants on the earth. We must take on the task of responsible stewardship, and these organizations provide a place to begin.

The organizations listed here are doing everything in their power to restore the earth and its waters. You can help by joining them in volunteer projects to clean streams of trash, building fish ladders, contributing to intelligent and thoughtful water-policy decisions, or by choosing to fish in ecologically responsible ways, such as catch-and-release, or with light tackle.

American Forestry Association
1319 18th Street, N.W.
Washington, D.C. 20016

American League of Anglers
810 18th Street, N.W.
Washington, D.C. 20016

American Medical Fly Fishing Association
7130 Morningside
Loomis, California 95650

American Rivers Conservation Council
317 Pennsylvania Avenue, S.E.
Washington D.C. 20003

American Rivers Touring Association
1016 Jackson Street
Oakland, California 94607

Appalachian Mountain Club
5 Joy Street
Boston, Massachusetts 02108

British Columbia Steelhead Society
Box 33947, Station D
Vancouver, British Columbia
Canada V6J 3J3

California Fisheries Restoration Foundation
1212 Broadway
Oakland, California 94612

California Trout Incorporated
Box 2046
San Francisco, California 94126

The Cousteau Society
7777 Third Avenue
New York, New York 10017

Defenders of Wildlife
2000 "N" Street, N.W.
Washington, D.C. 20036

Environmental Defense Fund
2728 Durant
Berkeley, California 94704

Conservation Organizations

The Environmental Planning Lobby
502 Park Avenue
New York, New York 10022

Environmental Policy Center
502 Pennsylvania Avenue, S.E.
Washington, D.C. 20003

The Federation of Fly Fishermen
Box 1088
West Yellowstone, Montana 59758

Foundation for Montana Trout
Box 652
Ennis, Montana 59729

Friends of the Earth
529 Commercial Street
San Francisco, California 94111

Friends of the Wilderness
3515 East Fourth Street
Duluth, Minnesota 55804

International Game Fish Association
3000 Las Olas Boulevard
Fort Lauderdale, Florida 33316

Isaak Walton League
1800 North Kent Street, Suite 806
Arlington, Virginia 22209

Michigan United Conservation Club
Box 2235
Lansing, Michigan 48911

National Audubon Society
950 Third Avenue
New York, New York 10022

National Wildlife Federation
1412 Sixth Street, N.W.
Washington, D.C. 20036

The Nature Conservancy
1800 North Kent Street
Arlington, Virginia 22209

Restoration of Atlantic Salmon in America,
Incorporated
Box 164
Hancock, New Hampshire 03449

Saltwater Fly Rodders of America
Box 304
Cape May Courthouse, New Jersey 08120

Sierra Club
530 Bush Street
San Francisco, California 94108

Theodore Gordon Flyfishers
24 East 39th Street
New York, New York 10016

Trout Unlimited
(Local chapters all over the United States
and Canada)
Box 1944
Washington, D.C. 20013

United Fly Tyers, Incorporated
Box 723
Boston, Massachusetts 02102

Wilderness Society
1901 Pennsylvania Avenue, N.W.
Washington, D.C. 20006

Wildlife Society
3900 Wisconsin Avenue, N.W., Suite 5176
Washington, D.C. 20016

World Wildlife Fund
1601 Connecticut Avenue, N.W.
Washington, D.C. 20009